SAS Publishing

Data Mining Using SAS® Enterprise Miner™: A Case Study Approach, Second Edition

The Power to Know.

The correct bibliographic citation for this manual is as follows: SAS Institute Inc. 2003. *Data Mining Using SAS® Enterprise Miner™: A Case Study Approach, Second Edition.* Cary, NC: SAS Institute Inc.

Data Mining Using SAS® Enterprise Miner™: A Case Study Approach, Second Edition

Contents

Introduction to SAS Enterprise Miner

Starting Enterprise Miner

To start Enterprise Miner, start SAS and then type **miner** on the SAS command bar. Submit the command by pressing the Return key or by clicking the check mark icon next to the command bar.

Alternatively, select from the main menu

Solutions ▶ Analysis ▶ Enterprise Miner

For more information, see *Getting Started with SAS Enterprise Miner*.

Setting Up the Initial Project and Diagram

Enterprise Miner organizes data analyses into projects and diagrams. Each project may have several process flow diagrams, and each diagram may contain several analyses. Typically each diagram contains an analysis of one data set.

Follow these steps to create a project.

1   From the SAS menu bar, select

2   Type a name for the project, such as My Project.

3   Select the **Client/server project** check box if necessary.

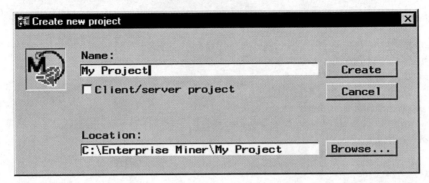

Note: You must have the access to a server that runs the same version of Enterprise Miner. For information about building a client/server project, see *Getting Started with SAS Enterprise Miner* or the online Help. △

4   Modify the location of the project folder by either typing a different location in the **Location** field or by clicking Browse.

5   Click Create. The project opens with an initial untitled diagram.

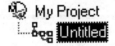

6   Select the diagram title and type a new name, such as My First Flow.

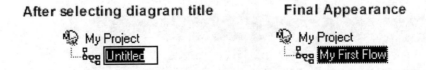

Identifying the Interface Components

The SAS Enterprise Miner window contains the following interface components:

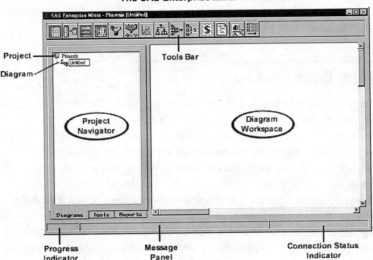

The SAS Enterprise Miner v.4 Window

- □ Project Navigator — enables you to manage projects and diagrams, add tools to the Diagram Workspace, and view HTML reports that are created by the Reporter node. Note that when a tool is added to the Diagram Workspace, the tool is referred to as a node. The Project Navigator has three tabs:

  - □ Diagrams tab — lists the current project and the diagrams within the project. By default, the project window opens with the Diagrams tab activated.

  - □ Tools tab — contains the Enterprise Miner tools palette. This tab enables you to see all of the tools (or nodes) that are available in Enterprise Miner. The tools are grouped according to the SEMMA data-mining methodology.

    Many of the commonly used tools are shown on the Tools Bar at the top of the window. You can add additional tools to the Tools Bar by dragging them from the Tools tab onto the Tools Bar. In addition, you can rearrange the tools on the Tools Bar by dragging each tool to a new location on the Tools Bar.

  - □ Reports tab — displays the HTML reports that are generated by using the Reporter node.

- □ Diagram Workspace — enables you to build, edit, run, and save process flow diagrams.

- □ Tools Bar — contains a customizable subset of Enterprise Miner tools that are commonly used to build process flow diagrams in the Diagram Workspace. You can add or delete tools from the Tools Bar.

- □ Progress Indicator — displays a progress indicator bar that indicates the execution status of an Enterprise Miner task.

- □ Message Panel — displays messages about the execution of an Enterprise Miner task.

- □ Connection Status Indicator — displays the remote host name and indicates whether the connection is active for a client/server project.

Data Mining and SEMMA

Definition of Data Mining

This document defines *data mining* as advanced methods for exploring and modeling relationships in large amounts of data.

Overview of the Data

Your data often comes from several different sources, and combining information from these different sources may present quite a challenge. The need for better and quicker access to information has generated a great deal of interest in building data warehouses that are able to quickly assemble and deliver the needed information in usable form. To download documentation that discusses the Enterprise Miner add-ins to SAS/Warehouse Administrator, go to the SAS Customer Support Center Web site (`http://support.sas.com`). From Software Downloads, select **Product and Solution Updates**. From the Demos and Downloads page, select **SAS/Warehouse Administrator Software**, and download the version that you want.

A typical data set has many thousand observations. An observation may represent an entity such as an individual customer, a specific transaction, or a certain household. Variables in the data set contain specific information such as demographic information, sales history, or financial information for each observation. How this information is used depends on the research question of interest.

When talking about types of data, consider the measurement level of each variable. You can generally classify each variable as one of the following:

- interval — a variable for which the mean (or average) makes sense, such as average income or average temperature.

- categorical — a variable consisting of a set of levels, such as gender (male or female) or drink size (small, regular, large). In general, if the variable is not continuous (that is, if taking the average does not make sense, such as average gender), then it is categorical. Categorical data can be grouped in several ways. For the purposes of Enterprise Miner, consider these subgroupings of categorical variables:

  - unary — a variable that has the same value for every observation in the data set.

  - binary — a variable that has only two possible levels. Gender is an example.

  - nominal — a variable that has more than two levels, but the values of the levels have no implied order. Pie flavors such as cherry, apple, and peach are examples.

  - ordinal — a variable that has more than two levels, and the values of the levels have an implied order. Drink sizes such as small, regular, and large are examples.

    Note: Ordinal variables may be treated as nominal variables, if you are not interested in the ordering of the levels. However, nominal variables cannot be treated as ordinal variables since there is no implied ordering by definition. △

  Missing values are not included in the counts.

To obtain a meaningful analysis, you must construct an appropriate data set and specify the correct measurement level for each of the variables.

Predictive and Descriptive Techniques

Predictive modeling techniques enable you to identify whether a set of input variables is useful in predicting some outcome variable. For example, a financial institution may try to determine if knowledge of an applicant's income and credit history (input variables) helps to predict whether the client is likely to default on a loan (outcome variable).

To distinguish the input variables from the outcome variables, set the model role for each variable in the data set. Identify outcome variables by using the target model role, and identify input variables by using the input model role. Examples of model roles include cost, freq, ID, and input. If you want to exclude some of the variables from the analysis, identify these variables by using the rejected model role. Specify a variable as an ID variable by using the ID model role.

Predictive modeling techniques require one or more outcome variables of interest. Each technique attempts to predict the outcome as well as possible according to some criteria such as maximizing accuracy or maximizing profit. This document shows you how to use several predictive modeling techniques through Enterprise Miner including regression models, decision trees, and neural networks. Each of these techniques enables you to predict a binary, nominal, ordinal, or continuous outcome variable from any combination of input variables.

Descriptive techniques enable you to identify underlying patterns in a data set. These techniques do not have a specific outcome variable of interest. This document explores how to use Enterprise Miner to perform the following descriptive analyses:

- □ Cluster analysis: This analysis attempts to find natural groupings of observations in the data, based on a set of input variables. After grouping the observations into clusters, you can use the input variables to try to characterize each group. When the clusters have been identified and interpreted, you can decide whether to treat each cluster independently.

- □ Association analysis: This analysis identifies groupings of products or services that tend to be purchased at the same time or at different times by the same customer. The analysis answers questions such as

    - □ What proportion of the people who purchased eggs and milk also purchased bread?

    - □ What proportion of the people who have a car loan with some financial institution later obtain a home mortgage from the same institution?

Overview of SEMMA

Enterprise Miner nodes are arranged into the following categories according the SAS process for data mining: SEMMA.

- □ Sample — identify input data sets (identify input data; sample from a larger data set; partition data set into training, validation, and test data sets).

- □ Explore — explore data sets statistically and graphically (plot the data, obtain descriptive statistics, identify important variables, perform association analysis).

- □ Modify — prepare the data for analysis (create additional variables or transform existing variables for analysis, identify outliers, replace missing values, modify the way in which variables are used for the analysis, perform cluster analysis, analyze data with self-organizing maps (known as SOMs) or Kohonen networks).

- □ Model — fit a predictive model (model a target variable by using a regression model, a decision tree, a neural network, or a user-defined model).

□ Assess — compare competing predictive models (build charts that plot the percentage of respondents, percentage of respondents captured, lift, and profit).

The Score and Score Converter nodes form another group, Score, and are designed to capture score code for the models and to translate the SAS DATA step score code into the C and Java programming languages. The SAS DATA step score code can be saved as a SAS program outside Enterprise Miner. The SAS program can then be run on any platform that runs base SAS. Thus, you can perform the actual scoring on almost any type of platform. Code that is based on the C or Java languages can be integrated into standalone C or Java programs that operate outside SAS.

Additional tools are available under the Utility nodes group.

Overview of the Nodes

Sample Nodes

Input Data Source

The Input Data Source node reads data sources and defines their attributes for later processing by Enterprise Miner. This node can perform various tasks:

□ access SAS data sets and data marts. Data marts can be defined by using the SAS Data Warehouse Administrator, and they can be set up for Enterprise Miner by using the Enterprise Miner Warehouse Add-ins.

□ automatically create a metadata sample for each variable when you import a data set with the Input Data Source node. By default, Enterprise Miner obtains the metadata sample by taking a random sample of 2,000 observations from the data set that is identified in the Input Data Source. Optionally, you can request larger samples. If the data is smaller than 2,000 observations, the entire data set is used

□ use the metadata sample to set initial values for the measurement level and the model role for each variable. You can change these values if you are not satisfied with the automatic selections that are made by the node.

□ display summary statistics for interval and class variables.

□ define target profiles for each target in the input data set.

Note: This document uses the term *data sets* instead of *data tables*. △

Sampling

The Sampling node enables you to perform random sampling, stratified random sampling, and cluster sampling. Sampling is recommended for extremely large databases because it can significantly decrease model-training time. If the sample is sufficiently representative, relationships that are found in the sample can be expected to generalize to the complete data set. The Sampling node writes the sampled observations to an output data set and saves the seed values that are used to generate the random numbers for the samples. You can replicate the samples by using the same seed value.

Data Partition

The Data Partition node enables you to partition data sets into training, test, and validation data sets. The training data set is used for preliminary model fitting. The validation data set is used to monitor and tune the model weights during estimation and is also used for model assessment. The test data set is an additional data set that you can use for model assessment. This node uses simple random sampling, stratified random sampling, or a user-defined partition to create training, test, or validation data sets. Specify a user-defined partition if you have determined which observations should be assigned to the training, validation, or test data sets. This assignment is identified by a categorical variable that is in the raw data set.

Explore Nodes

Distribution Explorer

The Distribution Explorer node enables you to explore large volumes of data in multidimensional histograms. You can view the distribution of up to three variables at a time with this node. When the variable is binary, nominal, or ordinal, you can select specific values to exclude from the chart. To exclude extreme values for interval variables, you can set a range cutoff. The node also generates simple descriptive statistics for the interval variables.

Multiplot

The Multiplot node enables you to explore large volumes of data graphically. Unlike the Insight or Distribution Explorer nodes, the Multiplot node automatically creates bar charts and scatter plots for the input and target variables without making several menu or window item selections. The code that is created by this node can be used to create graphs in a batch environment, whereas the Insight and Distribution Explorer nodes must be run interactively.

Insight

The Insight node enables you to open a SAS/INSIGHT session. SAS/INSIGHT software is an interactive tool for data exploration and analysis. With it, you explore samples of data through graphs and analyses that are linked across multiple windows. You can analyze univariate distributions, investigate multivariate distributions, and fit explanatory models by using generalized linear models.

Association

The Association node enables you to identify association relationships within the data. For example, if a customer buys a loaf of bread, how likely is the customer to buy a gallon of milk as well? The node also enables you to perform sequence discovery if a time-stamp variable (a sequence variable) is present in the data set.

Variable Selection

The Variable Selection node enables you to evaluate the importance of input variables in predicting or classifying the target variable. To select the important inputs, the node uses either an R-square or a Chi-square selection (tree-based) criterion. The R-square criterion enables you to remove variables that have large percentages of missing values, remove class variables that are based on the number of unique values, and remove variables in hierarchies. Variables can be hierarchical because of levels of generalization (Zipcode generalizes to State, which generalizes to Region) or because of formulation (variable A and variable B may have interaction A*B). The variables that are not related to the target are set to a status of rejected. Although rejected variables are passed to subsequent nodes in the process flow diagram, these variables are not used as model inputs by more detailed modeling nodes, such as the Neural Network and Tree nodes. Certain variables of interest may be rejected by a variable selection technique, but you can force these variables into the model by reassigning the input model role to these variables in any modeling node.

Link Analysis

The Link Analysis node enables you to tranform data from different sources into a data model that can be graphed. The data model supports simple statistical measures, presents a simple interactive graph for basic analytical exploration, and generates cluster scores from raw data. The scores can be used for data reduction and segmentation.

Modify Nodes

Data Set Attributes

The Data Set Attributes node enables you to modify data set attributes, such as data set names, descriptions, and roles. You can also use this node to modify the metadata sample that is associated with a data set and to specify target profiles for a target. An example of a useful Data Set Attributes application is to generate a data set in the SAS Code node and then modify its metadata sample with this node.

Transform Variables

The Transform Variables node enables you to transform variables; for example, you can transform variables by taking the square root of a variable, by taking the natural logarithm, maximizing the correlation with the target, or normalizing a variable. Additionally, the node supports user-defined formulas for transformations and enables you to group interval-valued variables into buckets or quantiles. This node also automatically places interval variables into buckets by using a decision tree-based algorithm. Transforming variables to similar scale and variability may improve the fit of models and, subsequently, the classification and prediction precision of fitted models.

Filter Outliers

The Filter Outliers node enables you to identify and remove outliers from data sets. Checking for outliers is recommended, as outliers may greatly affect modeling results and, subsequently, the classification and prediction precision of fitted models.

Replacement

The Replacement node enables you to impute (fill in) values for observations that have missing values. You can replace missing values for interval variables with the mean, median, midrange, mid-minimum spacing, or distribution-based replacement, or you can use a replacement M-estimator such as Tukey's biweight, Huber's, or Andrew's Wave. You can also estimate the replacement values for each interval input by using a tree-based imputation method. Missing values for class variables can be replaced with the most frequently occurring value, distribution-based replacement, tree-based imputation, or a constant.

Clustering

The Clustering node enables you to segment your data; that is, it enables you to identify data observations that are similar in some way. Observations that are similar tend to be in the same cluster, and observations that are different tend to be in different clusters. The cluster identifier for each observation can be passed to other nodes for use as an input, ID, or target variable. It can also be passed as a group variable that enables you to automatically construct separate models for each group.

SOM/Kohonen

The SOM/Kohonen node generates self-organizing maps, Kohonen networks, and vector quantization networks. Essentially the node performs unsupervised learning in which it attempts to learn the structure of the data. As with the Clustering node, after the network maps have been created, the characteristics can be examined graphically by using the Results browser. The node provides the analysis results in the form of an interactive map that illustrates the characteristics of the clusters. Furthermore, it provides a report that indicates the importance of each variable.

Time Series

The Time Series node enables you to convert transactional data to time series data. It also performs seasonal and trend analysis on time-stamped transactional data.

Interactive Grouping

The Interactive Grouping node enables you to interactively group variable values into classes. Statistical and plotted information can be interactively rearranged as you explore various variable groupings. The Interactive Grouping node requires a binary target variable.

Model Nodes

Regression

The Regression node enables you to fit both linear and logistic regression models to your data. You can use both continuous and discrete variables as inputs. The node supports the stepwise, forward, and backward-selection methods. A point-and-click interaction builder enables you to create higher-order modeling terms.

Tree

The Tree node enables you to perform multiway splitting of your database, based on nominal, ordinal, and continuous variables. This is the SAS implementation of decision trees, which represents a hybrid of the best of CHAID, CART, and C4.5 algorithms. The node supports both automatic and interactive training. When you run the Tree node in automatic mode, it automatically ranks the input variables by the strength of their contribution to the tree. This ranking can be used to select variables for use in subsequent modeling. In addition, dummy variables can be generated for use in subsequent modeling. Using interactive training, you can override any automatic step by defining a splitting rule or by pruning a node or subtree.

Neural Network

The Neural Network node enables you to construct, train, and validate multilayer feed-forward neural networks. By default, the Neural Network node automatically constructs a multilayer feed-forward network that has one hidden layer consisting of three neurons. In general, each input is fully connected to the first hidden layer, each hidden layer is fully connected to the next hidden layer, and the last hidden layer is fully connected to the output. The Neural Network node supports many variations of this general form.

Princomp/
Dmneural

The Princomp/Dmneural node enables you to fit an additive nonlinear model that uses the bucketed principal components as inputs to predict a binary or an interval target variable. The node also performs a principal components analysis and passes the principal components to the successor nodes.

User
Defined
Model

The User Defined Model node enables you to generate assessment statistics by using predicted values from a model that you built with the SAS Code node (for example, a logistic model that uses the SAS/STAT LOGISTIC procedure) or the Variable Selection node. You can also generate assessment statistics for models that are built by a third-party software product when you create a SAS data set that contains the predicted values from the model. The predicted values can also be saved to a SAS data set and then imported into the process flow with the Input Data Source node.

Ensemble

The Ensemble node creates a new model by averaging the posterior probabilities (for class targets) or the predicted values (for interval targets) from multiple models. The new model is then used to score new data. One common approach is to resample the training data and fit a separate model for each sample. The Ensemble node then integrates the component models to form a potentially stronger solution. Another common approach is to use multiple modeling methods, such as a neural network and a decision tree, to obtain separate models from the same training data set.

The Ensemble node integrates the component models from the complementary modeling methods to form the final model solution. The Ensemble node can also be used to combine the scoring code from stratified models. The modeling nodes generate different scoring formulas when they operate on a stratification variable (for example, a group variable such as Gender) that you define in a Group Processing node. The Ensemble node combines the scoring code into a single DATA step by logically dividing the data into blocks by using IF-THEN DO/END statements.

It is important to note that the ensemble model that is created from either approach can be more accurate than the individual models only if the individual models differ.

Memory-Based Reasoning

The Memory-Based Reasoning node is a modeling tool that uses a k-nearest neighbor algorithm to categorize or predict observations.

Two Stage Model

The Two Stage Model node computes a two-stage model to predict a class target and an interval target. The interval target variable is usually a value that is associated with a level of the class target variable.

Assess Nodes

Assessment

The Assessment node provides a common framework for comparing models and predictions from any of the modeling nodes (Regression, Tree, Neural Network, and User Defined Model nodes). The comparison is based on the expected and actual profits or losses that would result from implementing the model. The node produces the following charts that help to describe the usefulness of the model: lift, profit, return on investment, receiver operating curves, diagnostic charts, and threshold-based charts.

Reporter

The Reporter node assembles the results from a process flow analysis into an HTML report that can be viewed with a Web browser. Each report contains header information, an image of the process flow diagram, and a separate report for each node in the flow including node settings and results. Reports are managed in the Reports tab of the Project Navigator.

Scoring Nodes

Score

The Score node enables you to generate and manage predicted values from a trained model. Scoring formulas are created for both assessment and prediction. Enterprise Miner generates and manages scoring formulas in the form of SAS DATA step code, which can usually be used in SAS even without the presence of Enterprise Miner.

Score Converter

The Score Converter node provides scored data mining output in both the C and Java languages. The choices of language output enable you to use Enterprise Miner output in programs that operate outside SAS.

Utility Nodes

Group Processing

The Group Processing node enables you to perform an analysis for each level of a class variable such as Gender. You can also use this node to specify multiple targets or process the same data source repeatedly. When multiple targets are selected, Enterprise Miner analyzes each target separately.

Data Mining Database

The Data Mining Database node enables you to create a data mining database (DMDB) for batch processing. For nonbatch processing, Enterprise Miner automatically creates DMDBs as they are needed.

SAS Code

The SAS Code node enables you to incorporate new or existing SAS code into process flow diagrams. You can also use a SAS DATA step to create customized scoring code, to conditionally process data, and to concatenate or to merge existing data sets. The node provides a macro facility to dynamically reference data sets (used for training, validation, testing, or for scoring) and variables, such as input, target, and predict variables. After you run the SAS Code node, you can then export the results and the data sets for use by subsequent nodes in the diagram.

Control point

The Control Point node enables you to establish a control point to reduce the number of connections that are made in process flow diagrams. For example, suppose that you want to connect three Input Data Source nodes to three modeling nodes. If you omit the Control Point node, then you need nine connections to connect all of the Input Data Source nodes to all of the modeling nodes. However, if you use the Control Point node, you need only six connections.

Subdiagram

The Subdiagram node enables you to group a portion of a process flow diagram into a subdiagram. For complex process flow diagrams, you may want to create subdiagrams to better design and control the process flow.

Some General Usage Rules for Nodes

These are some general rules that govern placing nodes in a process flow diagram:

- ☐ The Input Data Source cannot be preceded by any other node.
- ☐ The Sampling node must be preceded by a node that exports a data set.
- ☐ The Assessment node must be preceded by one or more model nodes.
- ☐ The Score node or Score Converter node must be preceded by a node that produces score code. Any node that modifies the data or builds models generates score code.
- ☐ The SAS Code node can be defined in any stage of the process flow diagram. It does not require an input data set to be defined in the Input Data Source node.

Accessing SAS Data through SAS Libraries

SAS uses libraries to organize files. These libraries point to folders where data and programs are stored. In Enterprise Miner, Release 4.2, libraries must conform to the SAS Version 8 naming conventions. These conventions require the library name to have no more than eight alphanumeric characters. The first character of the name must be a letter or an underscore (_). Subsequent characters can be characters, numeric digits, and underscores. The name cannot contain special characters such as asterisks (*) and ampersands (&). For more information, see Names in the SAS Language in SAS Help and Documentation.

To create a new library or to view existing libraries, select from the main SAS menu

The following display shows an example of the Explorer window.

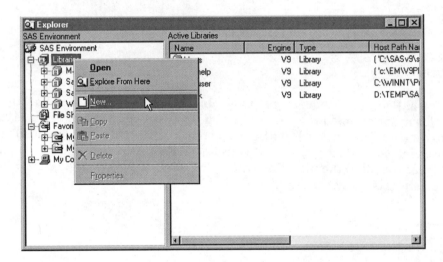

You can view the files in a library by selecting the library name from the list of libraries in the left panel of the Explorer window. To create a new library, right-click **Libraries** and select **New**. The New Library window opens.

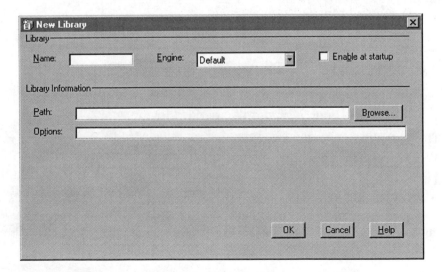

Specify the library name, engine, associated path, and options.

In the display, the **Enable at Startup** check box is not selected. This library will not be reassigned every time that the SAS session starts. Select the check box if you want SAS to automatically assign the library each time SAS starts.

Several libraries are automatically assigned when you start Enterprise Miner. One of these libraries (SAMPSIO) contains sample data sets that are used in Enterprise Miner reference material. This document uses the data sets that are in SAMPSIO. Any data set in the library can then be referenced by the two-part name that is constructed by using the SAS library name and the SAS data set name. For example, the HMEQ data set in the SAMPSIO library is identified by the two-part name SAMPSIO.HMEQ.

CHAPTER

2

Predictive Modeling

Problem Formulation

Overview of the Predictive Modeling Case

A financial services company offers a home equity line of credit to its clients. The company has extended several thousand lines of credit in the past, and many of these accepted applicants (approximately 20%) have defaulted on their loans. By using geographic, demographic, and financial variables, the company wants to build a model to predict whether an applicant will default.

Input Data Source

After analyzing the data, the company selected a subset of 12 predictor (or input) variables to model whether each applicant defaulted. The response (or target) variable (BAD) indicates whether an applicant defaulted on the home equity line of credit. These variables, along with their model role, measurement level, and description, are shown in the following table.

Note: This book uses uppercase for variable names. SAS accepts mixed case and lowercase variable names as well. △

Table 2.1 Variables in the SAMPSIO.HMEQ Data Set

Name	Model Role	Measurement Level	Description
BAD	Target	Binary	1=applicant defaulted on loan or seriously delinquent, 0=applicant paid loan
CLAGE	Input	Interval	Age of oldest credit line in months
CLNO	Input	Interval	Number of credit lines
DEBTINC	Input	Interval	Debt-to-income ratio
DELINQ	Input	Interval	Number of delinquent credit lines
DEROG	Input	Interval	Number of major derogatory reports
JOB	Input	Nominal	Occupational categories
LOAN	Input	Interval	Amount of the loan request
MORTDUE	Input	Interval	Amount due on existing mortgage
NINQ	Input	Interval	Number of recent credit inquiries
REASON	Input	Binary	DebtCon=debt consolidation. HomeImp=home improvement

Name	Model Role	Measurement Level	Description
VALUE	Input	Interval	Value of current property
YOJ	Input	Interval	Years at present job

The HMEQ data set in the SAMPSIO library contains 5,960 observations for building and comparing competing models. The data set is split into training, validation, and test data sets for analysis.

Creating a Process Flow Diagram

Adding the Nodes

Begin building the first flow to analyze this data. Use the Enterprise Miner Tools Bar to access the commonly used nodes. You can add additional nodes to the Tools Bar by dragging the nodes from the Tools tab of the Project Navigator to the Tools Bar. All of the nodes will remain available in the Tools tab.

Add an Input Data Source node by dragging the node from the Tools Bar or from the Tools tab of the Project Navigator. Because this is a predictive modeling flow, add a Data Partition node to the right of the Input Data Source node. In addition to dragging a node onto the Diagram Workspace, there are two other ways to add a node to the flow. You can right-click in the workspace in which you want the node to appear and select **Add node**, or you can double-click where you want the node to appear. In all cases, a list of nodes appears for you to choose from. After you select Data Partition, your diagram should look as follows.

Input Data
Source

Data
Partition

Observe that the Data Partition node is selected (as indicated by the dotted line around it) but the Input Data Source node is not. If you click in any open space on the workspace, all nodes become deselected.

Using the Cursor

The shape of the cursor changes depending on where it is positioned. The behavior of the mouse commands depends on the shape of the cursor as well as on the selection state of the node over which the cursor is positioned. Right-click in an open area to see the pop-up menu as shown below.

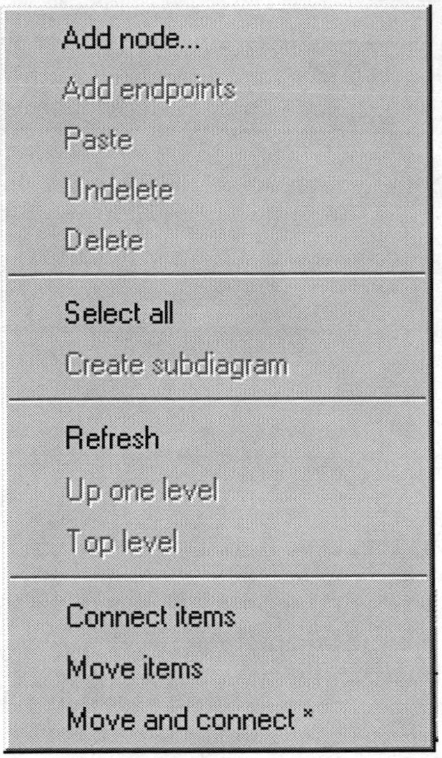

Add node...

Add endpoints

Paste

Undelete

Delete

Select all

Create subdiagram

Refresh

Up one level

Top level

Connect items

Move items

Move and connect *

The last three menu items (**Connect items**, **Move items**, **Move and connect**) enable you to modify the ways in which the cursor may be used. The **Move and connect** item is selected by default as indicated by the asterisk (*) that appears next to it. It is recommended that you do not change this setting, as it is more convenient and efficient to use the mouse to perform both tasks without the need to toggle between cursor settings. If your cursor is not performing a task, check this menu to make sure that the **Move and connect** item is selected. This selection enables you to move the nodes around the workspace as well as to connect them.

Note that after you drag a node, the node remains selected. To deselect all of the nodes, click in an open area of the workspace. Also note that when you put the cursor on the outside edge of the node, the cursor appears as a cross-hair. You can connect the node where the cursor is positioned (beginning node) to any other node (ending node) as follows:

1   Ensure that the beginning node is deselected. It is much easier to drag a line when the node is deselected. If the beginning node is selected, click in an open area of the workspace to deselect it.

2   Position the cursor on the edge of the icon that represents the beginning node (until the cross-hair appears).

3   Press the left mouse button and immediately begin to drag in the direction of the ending node. Note: If you do not begin dragging immediately after pressing the left mouse button, you will only select the node. Dragging a selected node will generally result in moving the node (that is, no line will form).

4   Release the mouse button after you reach the edge of the icon that represents the ending node.

5   Click away from the arrow. Initially, the connection will appear as follows. After you click away from the line in an open area of the workspace, the finished arrow forms.

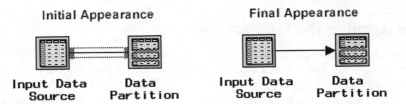

Initial Appearance   Final Appearance

Input Data   Data   Input Data   Data
Source   Partition   Source   Partition

Identifying the Input Data

The first example uses the HMEQ data set in the SAMPSIO library. To specify the input data, double-click the Input Data Source node or right-click this node and select **Open**. The Data tab is active. Your window should look like the one below.

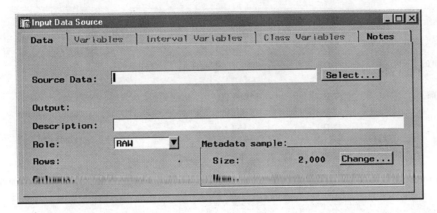

Click [Select] in order to select the data set. Alternatively, you can type the name of the data set.

The SASUSER library is selected by default. To view data sets in the SAMPSIO

library, click the arrow (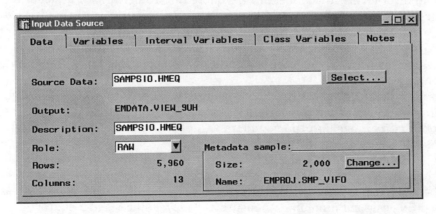) and select SAMPSIO from the list of defined libraries.

Select the HMEQ data set from the list of data sets in the SAMPSIO library, and then select [OK]. The Input Data Source dialog box appears.

Observe that this data set has 5,960 observations (rows) and 13 variables (columns). The name of the source data set is SAMPSIO.HMEQ. You could have typed in this name instead of selecting it through the dialog box. Note that the lower-right corner indicates a metadata sample of size 2,000.

Understanding the Metadata Sample

All analysis packages must determine how to use variables in the analysis. Enterprise Miner uses metadata in order to make a preliminary assessment of how to use each variable. By default, it takes a random sample of 2,000 observations from the data set of interest, and uses this information to assign a model role and a measurement level to each variable. It also computes simple descriptive statistics that are displayed under additional tabs. If you want to take a larger sample, you may select Change in the metadata sample area of the window (lower right corner), but this change is unnecessary in most cases, and it is not shown here.

Evaluate (and update, if necessary) the assignments that were made using the metadata sample. Select the Variables tab to see all of the variables and their respective assignments. You can see all of the variables if you maximize the window. The following table shows a portion of the information for each of the 13 variables in this example.

Name	Model Role	Measurement	Type	Format	Informat
BAD	target	binary	num	BEST12.	12.
LOAN	input	interval	num	BEST12.	12.
MORTDUE	input	interval	num	BEST12.	12.
VALUE	input	interval	num	BEST12.	12.
REASON	input	binary	char	$7.	$7.
JOB	input	nominal	char	$7.	$7.
YOJ	input	interval	num	BEST12.	12.
DEROG	input	interval	num	BEST12.	12.
DELINQ	input	ordinal	num	BEST12.	12.
CLAGE	input	interval	num	BEST12.	12.
NINQ	input	interval	num	BEST12.	12.
CLNO	input	interval	num	BEST12.	12.
DEBTINC	input	interval	num	BEST12.	12.

Observe that values in the **Name** and **Type** columns are not available (they appear dimmed). These columns represent information from the SAS data set that cannot be modified in this node. The name must conform to the naming conventions that are described earlier for libraries. The type is either character **(char)** or numeric **(num)** and affects how a variable can be used. Enterprise Miner uses the value for **Type** and the number of levels in the metadata sample to initially assign a model role and measurement level to each variable.

The first variable listed is BAD. Although BAD is a numeric variable in the data set, Enterprise Miner identifies it as a binary variable since it has only two distinct nonmissing levels in the metadata sample. The model role for all binary variables is set to **input** by default.

The next three variables (LOAN, MORTDUE, and VALUE) are assigned an interval measurement level since they are numeric variables in the SAS data set and have more than ten distinct levels in the metadata sample. The model role for all interval variables is set to **input** by default.

The variables REASON and JOB are both character variables in the data set, yet they have different measurement levels. REASON is assigned a binary measurement level because it has only two distinct nonmissing levels in the metadata sample. JOB, however, is assigned a nominal measurement level since it is a character variable with more than two levels. The model role for all binary and nominal variables is set to input by default.

In the table, DELINQ has been assigned an ordinal measurement level. The assignment of an ordinal measurement level occurs when each is a numeric variable with more than two, but not more than ten, distinct nonmissing levels in the metadata sample. This often occurs in variables that contain counts (such as number of children). Since this assignment depends on the number of levels for each variable in the metadata sample, the measurement level of DEROG or DELINQ for the analysis may be set to interval. For the purpose of this analysis, treat the remaining variables (YOJ through DEBTINC) as interval variables.

Identifying Target Variables

Because BAD is the response variable for this analysis, change the model role for BAD to target. To modify the model role information for BAD, proceed as follows:

1 Right–click in the **Model Role** column of the row for BAD.

2 Select

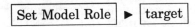

Set Model Role ▶ target

from the pop-up menu.

Inspecting Distribution

You can inspect the distribution of values in the metadata sample for each of the variables. To view the distribution of BAD, for example, proceed as follows:

1 Right-click in the **Name** column for the variable BAD.

2 Select **View distribution** to see the distribution of values for BAD in the metadata sample. Here is an example distribution.

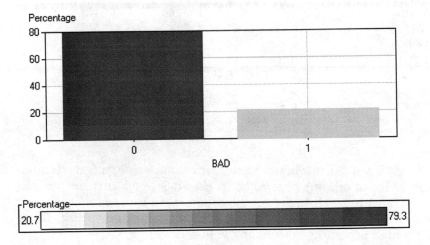

To obtain additional information, select the View Info icon ( ) from the toolbox at the top of the window and click one of the histogram bars. Enterprise Miner displays the level and the proportion of observations that are represented by the bar. These plots provide an initial overview of the data. For this example, approximately 20% of the observations were loans for which the client defaulted (BAD=1).

Recall that the plots and statistics in the Input Data Source node are based on the metadata sample, so the exact values in your window may differ slightly from those displayed here. These differences will not appear later in the modeling results since the modeling nodes use the entire training data set and not just a sample.

Select Close to return to the main dialog box when you are finished inspecting the plot.

Modifying Variable Information

Ensure that the remaining variables have the correct model role and measurement level information as shown in Table 2.1. If necessary, change the measurement level for DEROG and DELINQ to **ordinal**. This is not done in this example.

To modify the measurement level information for DEROG, proceed as follows:

1 Right-click the **Measurement Level** column of the row for DEROG.

2 Select

| Set Measurement Level | ▶ | ordinal |

3 Repeat steps 1 and 2 for DELINQ.

Alternatively, you could have updated the model role information for both variables simultaneously by selecting the rows for both DEROG and DELINQ before following steps 1 and 2.

Investigating Descriptive Statistics

The metadata is used to compute descriptive statistics. Select the Interval Variables tab.

Name	Min	Max	Mean	Std Dev.	Missing %
LOAN	1700	89900	18655	11334	0%
MORTDUE	2063	399550	74869	46643	8%
VALUE	8000	855909	103344	65121	3%
YOJ	0	41	8.7173	7.5321	8%
DEROG	0	10	0.2813	0.9023	12%
DELINQ	0	10	0.4472	1.1168	10%
CLAGE	0	649.75	181.69	86.96	5%
NINQ	0	12	1.2129	1.72	8%
CLNO	0	71	21.192	10.063	3%
DEBTINC	0.5245	143.95	33.843	8.2244	22%

Investigate the minimum value, maximum value, mean, standard deviation, percentage of missing observations, skewness, and kurtosis for interval variables. You might need to scroll to see all the columns. In this example, an inspection of the minimum and maximum values indicates no unusual values. Observe that DEBTINC has a high percentage of missing values (22%).

Select the Class Variables tab.

Name	Values	Missing %	Order
BAD	2	0%	Descending
REASON	2	4%	Ascending
JOB	6	4%	Ascending

Investigate the number of levels, percentage of missing values, and the sort order of each variable. The sort order for BAD is descending, but the sort order for all the others is ascending. For a binary target such as BAD, the first sorted level is the target event. Since BAD has two levels (0 and 1) and BAD is sorted in descending order, BAD=1 is the target event. You might need to change the sort order to get the target event that you want. Close the Input Data Source node, and save changes when you are prompted.

Inspecting Default Settings in the Data Partition Node

Open the Data Partition node. The Partition tab is active by default. The partition method options are found in the upper-left corner of the Partition tab.

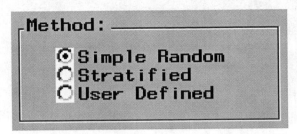

Enterprise Miner takes a sample of the input data and divides it into training, validation, and test data sets. By default, simple random sampling is used. You can generate stratified samples or implement previously implemented user-defined samples as follows.

□ simple random sampling — Select **Simple Random**. Every observation in the data set has the same probability to be selected.

□ stratified sampling — Select **Stratified** and then use the options in the Stratified tab to set up your strata.

□ user defined sampling — Select **User Defined** and then use the options in the User Defined tab to identify the variable in the data set that identifies the partitions.

The lower-left corner of the tab enables you to specify a random seed for initializing the sampling process. Randomization within computer programs is often started by some type of seed. If you use the same data set with the same seed (except seed=0) in different flows, you get the same partition. Observe that re-sorting the data results in a different ordering of data. Therefore, a different partition yields potentially different results.

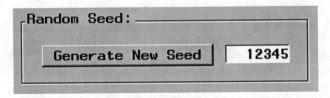

The right side of the tab enables you to specify the percentage of the data to allocate to training, validation, and test data. The percentages must add up to 100%.

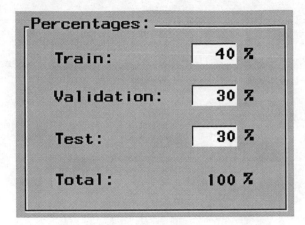

Use the default settings for this example. Close the Data Partition node. If you did not make changes, you will not be prompted to save changes. If you are prompted to save changes when you close this node, select No to retain the default settings of the Data Partition node.

Fitting and Evaluating a Regression Model

Add a Regression node and connect it from the Data Partition node. The diagram now appears as follows:

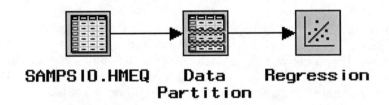

SAMPSIO.HMEQ   Data   Regression
                Partition

Modeling nodes, such as the Regression node, require you to specify a target variable in the Input Data Source node. The Regression node fits models for interval, ordinal, nominal, and binary targets. Since you selected a binary variable (BAD) as the target in the Input Data Source node, the Regression node will fit (by default) a binary logistic regression model with main effects for each input variable. The node also codes your grouping variables with either GLM coding or Deviation coding. By default, the node uses Deviation coding for categorical input variables.

Right-click the Regression node and select **Run**. When the run is complete, click Yes when you are prompted to view the results. The Estimates tab in the Regression Results Browser displays bar charts of effect T-scores and parameter estimates. The T-scores are plotted (from left to right) in decreasing order of their absolute values. The higher the absolute value is, the more important the variable is in the regression model. In this example, the variables DELINQ, NINQ, DEBTINC, and DEROG are the most important model predictors.

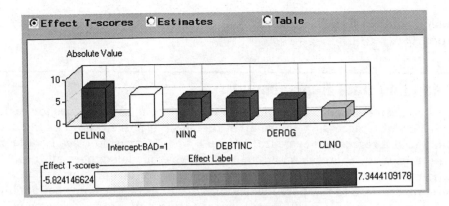

To view the effect T-scores and parameter estimates in a table, select **Table**.

All the modeling nodes have a Model Manager that enables you to produce the assessment charts and reports as the Assessment node. In the Model Manager, you are restricted to comparing models that are trained by the respective modeling node. In the Assessment node, you can compare models that are created from different modeling nodes.

Right-click the Regression node in the Diagram Workspace and select **Model Manager**. In the Model Manager, select

| Tools | ► | Lift Chart |

A cumulative %Response chart appears. By default, this chart arranges observations (individuals) into deciles based on their predicted probability of response, and then plots the actual percentage of respondents.

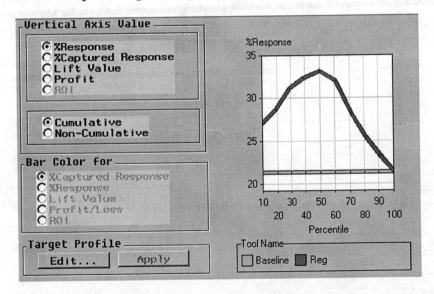

For this example, the individuals are sorted in descending order of their predicted probability of default on a loan. The plotted values are the cumulative actual probabilities of loan defaults. If the model is useful, the proportion of individuals that defaulted on a loan will be relatively high in the top deciles and the plotted curve will be decreasing. In this example, the default regression is not useful.

Recall that the variable DEBTINC has a high percentage of missing values. Applying a default regression model directly to the training data set is not appropriate in this example, because regression models ignore observations that have a missing value for at least one input variable. You should consider performing imputation before fitting a regression model. In Enterprise Miner, you can use the Replacement node to perform imputation.

Understanding Data Replacement

Add a Replacement node. This allows you to replace missing values for each variable. This replacement is necessary to use all of the observations in the training data set when you build a regression or neural network model. Decision trees handle missing values directly, while regression and neutral network models ignore all incomplete observations (observations that have a missing value for one or more input variables). It is more appropriate to compare models that are built on the same set of observations, so you should perform this replacement before fitting any regression or neural network model when you plan to compare the results to those obtained from a decision tree model.

By default, Enterprise Miner uses a sample from the training data set to select the values for replacement. The following statements are true:

☐ Observations that have a missing value for an interval variable have the missing value replaced with the mean of the sample for the corresponding variable.

☐ Observations that have a missing value for a binary, nominal, or ordinal variable have the missing value replaced with the most commonly occurring nonmissing level of the corresponding variable in the sample.

Your new diagram should appear as follows:

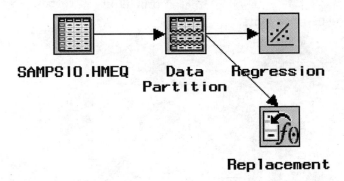

Fitting and Evaluating a Regression Model with Data Replacement

Add a Regression node and connect it from the Replacement node. Then, add an Assessment node. Your flow should now look as follows:

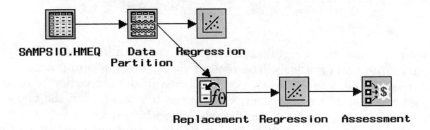

Right-click the Assessment node and select **Run**. Observe that each node becomes green as it runs. Since you ran the flow from the Assessment node, you will be prompted to see the Assessment results when Enterprise Miner completes its processing. View the results when you are prompted and select

| Tools | ► | Lift Chart |

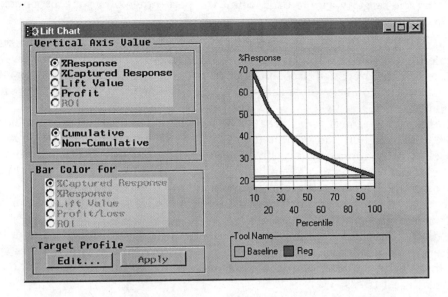

A cumulative %Response chart appears first. By default, this chart arranges individuals into deciles based on their predicted probability of response, and then plots the actual percentage of respondents. To see actual values, select the View Info icon

( ) from the toolbox and then click anywhere on the red line. Clicking on the red line near the upper-left corner of the plot indicates a %response of 67.56.

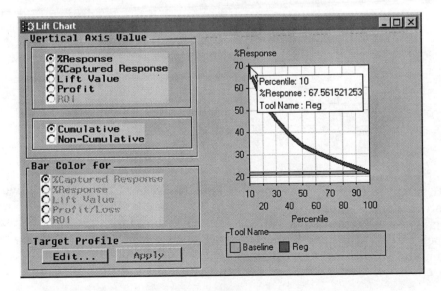

To interpret the cumulative %Response chart, consider how the chart is constructed.

1 For this example, the response of interest is loan defaults; thus, a respondent is defined as a individual who defaults on a loan (BAD=1). For each individual, the fitted model (in this case, a regression model) predicts the probability that the individual will default. The observations are sorted by the predicted probability of

response from the highest probability of response to the lowest probability of response.

2 The observations are then grouped into ordered bins, each containing approximately 10% of the data.

3 Using the target variable BAD, count the percentage of actual respondents in each bin.

If the model is useful, the proportion of individuals who have the event level that you are modeling (in this example, those who defaulted on a loan) will be relatively high in bins in which the predicted probability of response is high. The cumulative response curve that is shown above plots the percentage of respondents, such as the top 10%, top 20%, and top 30%.

In the top 10%, almost two-thirds of the individuals had defaulted on a loan. In the top 20%, just over half had defaulted on the loan. The horizontal blue line represents the baseline rate (approximately 20%) for comparison purposes. The baseline is an estimate of the percentage of defaulters that you would expect if you were to take a random sample. The default plot represents cumulative percentages, but you can also see the proportion of those who defaulted in each bin by selecting **Non-Cumulative** on the left side of the graph.

The discussion of the remaining charts refers to those who defaulted on a loan as defaulters or respondents. In the previous plot, the percentage of defaulters was 67.56% in the first decile. In other words, 67.56% of those in the first decile had the target event of interest (BAD=1).

Select **Non-Cumulative** and inspect the resulting plot.

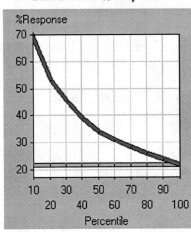

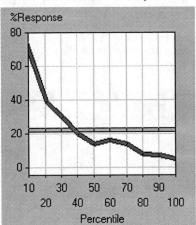

Both plots are displayed to allow further comparison. The noncumulative plot shows the percentage of defaulters in each decile. The cumulative plot can be obtained from averaging the appropriate percentages in the noncumulative plot. For example, the 20th percentile in the cumulative %Response plot can be calculated from averaging the non-cumulative percent response in the top two deciles of the non-cumulative %Response plot. Next select **Cumulative** and then select **Lift Value**.

Cumulative %Response   Cumulative Lift Value

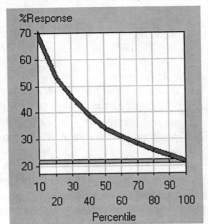 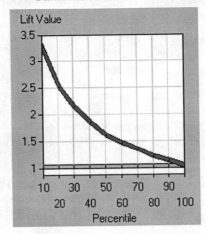

Lift charts plot the same information on a different scale. The overall response rate is 20%. Calculate lift by dividing the response rate in a given group by the overall response rate. The percentage of respondents in the first decile was 67.56%. Dividing 67.56% by 20% (overall response rate) gives a lift slightly higher than three, which indicates that the response rate in the first decile is over three times as high as the response rate in the population.

Instead of asking the question, "What percentage of those in a bin were defaulters?" you could ask the question, "What percentage of the total number of defaulters are in a bin?" The latter question can be evaluated by using the Captured Response curve. To inspect this curve, select **%Captured Response**. Use the View Info tool icon to evaluate how the model performs.

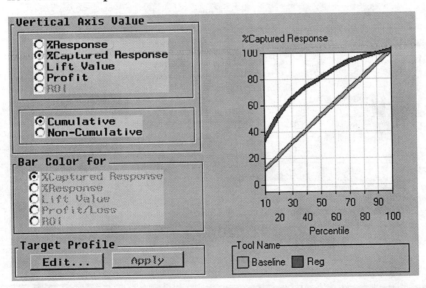

You can calculate lift from this type of chart as well. If you were to take a random sample of 10% of the observations, you would expect to capture 10% of the defaulters. Likewise, if you take a random sample of 20% of the data, you would expect to capture 20% of the defaulters. You can calculate lift, therefore, by dividing the proportion of the defaulters that you have captured by the percentage of those whom you have chosen for action (rejection of the loan application).

Observe that if the percentage of applications that were chosen for rejection were approximately 20% or 30%, one of the following conditions would be true.

□ If the value is 20%, you would have identified about 50% of those who would have defaulted, which corresponds to a lift of about 50/20=2.5.

□ If the value is 30%, you would have identified over 60% of those who would have defaulted, which corresponds to a lift of over 60/30=2.

Observe that lift depends on the proportion of those who have been chosen for action. Lift generally decreases as you choose larger and larger proportions of the data for action. When comparing two models on the same proportion of the data, the model that has the higher lift is often preferred (barring issues that involve model complexity and interpretability).

Note: A model that performs best in the one decile may perform poorly in other deciles; therefore, when you compare competing models, your choice of the final model may depend on the proportion of individuals that you have chosen for action.   △

You also can access the model results from an opened Assessment node. To do this, select from the main menu of an opened Assessment node

| View | ▶ | Model Results |

The Regression Results Browser opens. The initial bar chart frame may not display all of the effects. To view all the effect T-Scores or estimates, select from the main menu

| Format | ▶ | Rescale Axes |

You can select the View Info icon (⬚) from the toolbox and then select a bar to view the effect label.

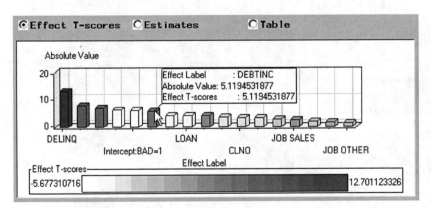

Now that imputation has been applied to the data set, variables DELINQ, DEROG, NINQ, CLAGE, and DEBTINC are the most important predictor variables.

Data Preparation and Investigation

Preliminary Investigation

Recall that the Insight node gives you access to many powerful statistical graphics that are useful for preliminary investigation. You can add an Insight node and connect it to the Data Partition node as follows.

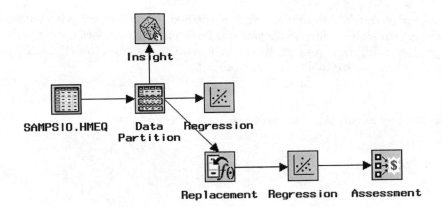

SAMPSIO.HMEQ   Data Partition   Regression

Insight

Replacement   Regression   Assessment

Run the flow from the Insight node by right-clicking the Insight node and selecting **Run**. Select **Yes** when you are prompted to see the results. A portion of the output is shown below.

▶ 13	Int	Int	Int	Int	Nom	Nom	Int
2000	BAD	LOAN	MORTDUE	VALUE	REASON	JOB	YOJ
1	1	1100	25860.00	39025.00	HomeImp	Other	10.50
2	1	1500	.	.			.
3	0	1700	97800.00	112000.00	HomeImp	Office	3.00
4	1	1800	48649.00	57037.00	HomeImp	Other	5.00
5	1	2000	20627.00	29800.00	HomeImp	Office	11.00
6	1	2000	45000.00	55000.00	HomeImp	Other	3.00
7	0	2000	64536.00	87400.00		Mgr	2.50
8	1	2200	90957.00	102600.00	HomeImp	Mgr	7.00
9	1	2200	23030.00	.			19.00
10	1	2300	20100.00	18150.00	HomeImp	Other	4.50

Observe that the upper-left corner contains the numbers 2000 and 17, which indicates there are 2,000 rows (observations) and 17 columns (variables). This represents a sample from either the training data set or the validation data set, but how would you know which one? Close the Insight node to return to the workspace.

Open the Insight node by right-clicking on the node in the workspace and selecting **Open**. The Data tab is initially active. An example is displayed below.

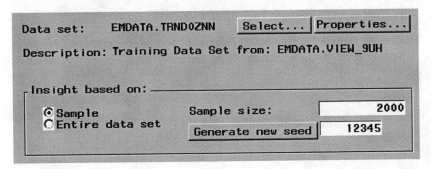

Observe that the selected data set is the training data set. The name of the data set, EMDATA.TRND0ZNN, is composed of key letters (in this case, TRN) and some random alphanumeric characters (in this case, D0ZNN) and is stored in the EMDATA library. The bottom of the tab indicates that Insight is generating a random sample of 2,000 observations from the training data based on the random seed 12345.

Since the naming process involves random assignment, the name of your data set will almost certainly be different; however, Enterprise Miner assigns the SAS library name EMDATA to the folder that contains these files. If you create a new project, these files will be placed in a different folder, but the SAS library name will still be EMDATA. This does not cause a conflict since you can have only one project open at one time. When opening a different project, Enterprise Miner reassigns the EMDATA library name to the appropriate folder for that project.

To change the data set that the Insight node is using, click [Select]. Inspect the resulting Imports Map dialog box.

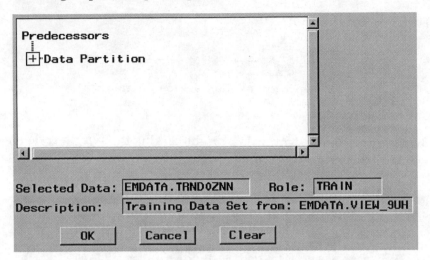

Data Partition is listed under Predecessors since the Data Partition node is connected to the Insight node. The Data Partition node is the only predecessor. Click the plus symbol ([+]) next to Data Partition and then click the ([+]) next to SAS_DATA_SETS. Three data sets are shown that represent the training (for example, TRND0ZNN), validation (for example, VALLTOB0), and test data sets (for example, TSTMUDA1).

If you click a SAS data set, the type of partition is displayed in the description field below the tree diagram.

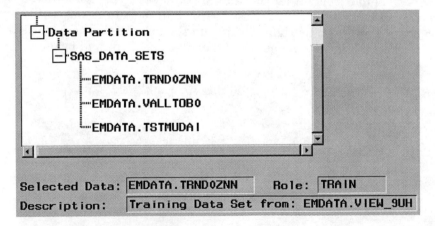

Select [OK] at the bottom of the Imports Map window to return to the Data tab.

> Data set: EMDATA.TRND0ZNN   [Select...] [Properties...]
>
> Description: Training Data Set from: EMDATA.VIEW_9UH

Click [Properties] in the Data tab as shown above. The Data Set Details window appears, and the Information tab is active. This tab provides information about when the data set was constructed as well as the number of rows and columns it contains. Select the Table View tab.

☑ Variable labels

	BAD	LOAN	MORTDUE	VALUE	REASON	JOB
1	1	1100	25860	39025	Homelmp	Other
2	1	1500	.	.		
3	0	1700	97800	112000	Homelmp	Office
4	1	1800	48649	57037	Homelmp	Other
5	1	2000	20627	29800	Homelmp	Office
6	1	2000	45000	55000	Homelmp	Other
7	0	2000	64536	87400		Mgr
8	1	2200	90957	102600	Homelmp	Mgr

This tab enables you to view the currently selected data set in tabular form. The check box enables you to see the column headings that use the variable labels. Deselecting the box would cause the table to use the SAS variable names for column headings. If no label is associated with the variable, the box displays the SAS variable name. Close the Data Set Details window when you are finished to return to the main Insight dialog box.

Select **Entire data set** to run the Insight node on the entire data set.

Note: Do not load extremely large data tables into the Insight node. If the data table is very large, using Insight on a moderate sample instead is usually sufficient to explore the data. △

To run the Insight node with the new settings:

1 Close the Insight dialog window.

2 Select ⌷Yes⌷ when you are prompted to save changes.

3 Run the diagram from the Insight node.

4 Select ⌷Yes⌷ when you are prompted to see the results.

Note: You can also run Insight without closing the Insight dialog box by selecting the Run icon (🏃) from the toolbox and selecting ⌷Yes⌷ when you are prompted to see the results. △

Before proceeding, check to ensure that the Insight window is the active window. From the menus at the top of Enterprise Miner, select

⌷ Window ⌷ ► ⌷ EMPROJ.SMP_TRN6 (in this example) ⌷

Investigate the distribution of each of the variables.

1 From the menus at the top of the Insight window, select

⌷ Analyze ⌷ ► ⌷ Distribution (Y) ⌷

2 Highlight all of the variables in the variable list.

3 Select **Y**.

4 Click ⌷OK⌷.

Charts for continuous variables include histograms, box and whisker plots, and assorted descriptive statistics. A portion of the output for the variable LOAN is shown below.

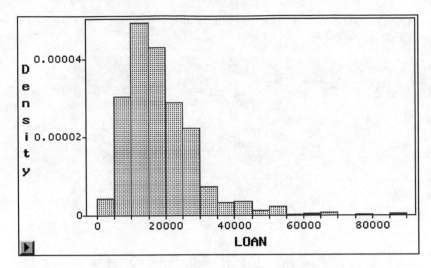

Moments			
N	2384.0000	Sum Wgts	2384.0000
Mean	18784.2282	Sum	44781600.0
Std Dev	11523.4590	Variance	132790108
Skewness	2.1647	Kurtosis	7.5583
USS	1.158E+12	CSS	3.164E+11
CV	61.3465	Std Mean	236.0096

Scroll through the output until you reach the graph for REASON. The unlabeled level represents observations that have a missing value for REASON.

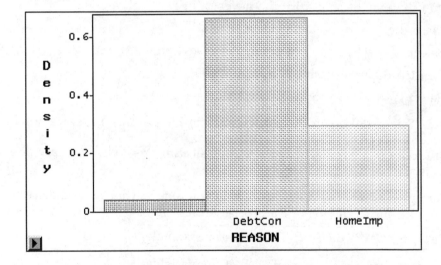

Now scroll down and inspect the distribution of YOJ (which is very skewed) and DEROG (which has a large proportion of observations at DEROG=0). Observe that DEROG has relatively few observations in which DEROG > 0.

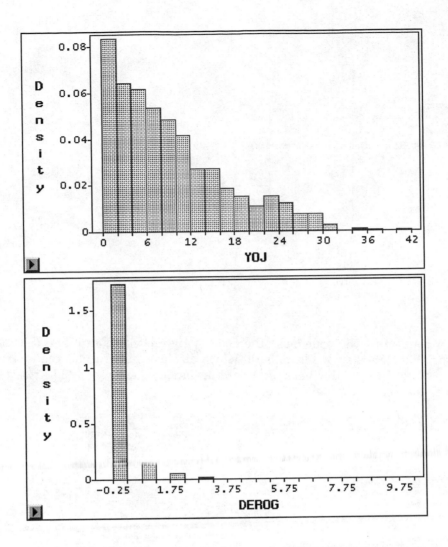

When you are finished, return to the main process flow diagram.

1 Close the distribution window when you are finished.

2 Close the Insight data table.

3 If you ran Insight without closing the node, close the Insight node (saving changes if you are prompted).

Performing Variable Transformation

After you have viewed the results in Insight, it will be clear that some input variables have highly skewed distributions. In highly skewed distributions, a small percentage of the points may have a great deal of influence. Sometimes, performing a transformation on an input variable can yield a better fitting model.

To do that, add a Transform Variables node as shown below.

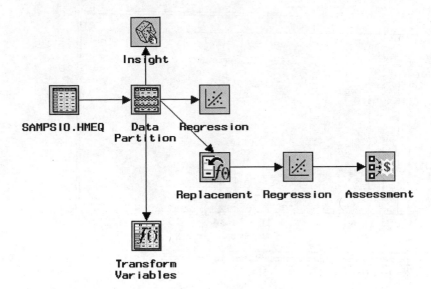

After connecting the node, open the node by right-clicking on it and selecting **Open**. The Variables tab is shown by default, which displays statistics for the interval level variables that include the mean, standard deviation, skewness, and kurtosis (calculated from the metadata sample).

Name	Keep	Role	Formula	Mean	Std Dev	Skew
LOAN	Yes	input		18816.9	11673.165628	2.1575215179
MORTDUE	Yes	input		73070.371208	43421.040999	1.5860264776
VALUE	Yes	input		101949.83349	58210.603775	3.3911486973
YOJ	Yes	input		8.7973097826	7.6384370166	1.0781332052
DEROG	Yes	input		0.2413987592	0.8286221978	5.8587447338
DELINQ	Yes	input		0.4532374101	1.2244732547	4.7406805248
CLAGE	Yes	input		181.53016351	87.547191047	1.6604951227
NINQ	Yes	input		1.148773842	1.6919826247	2.688970864
CLNO	Yes	input		21.125194805	10.23641608	0.8160567974
DEBTINC	Yes	input		33.891762201	9.4603236863	5.0238291442

The Transform Variables node enables you to rapidly transform interval valued variables by using standard transformations. You can also create new variables whose values are calculated from existing variables in the data set. Observe that the only available column in this dialog box is the Keep column. You can edit formulas for calculated columns by right-clicking the appropriate row or by using the **Actions** main menu.

You can view the distribution of each variable just as you did in the Input Data Source node. Right-click the row of YOJ and select **View Distribution**. Begin by viewing the distribution of YOJ.

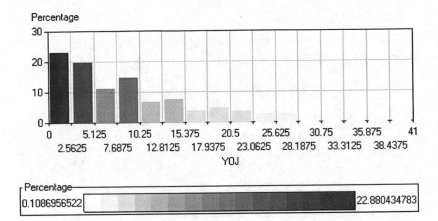

Consider a log transformation of YOJ. This transformation is one of several one-step transformations that are available in the Transform Variables node. After closing the graph of YOJ, create a new variable by taking the log of YOJ.

1 Position your cursor over the row for YOJ.

2 Right-click and select

3 Observe that a new variable has been added to the dialog box.

Name	Keep	Role	Formula	Mean	Std Dev
LOAN	Yes	input		18816.9	11673.165628
MORTDUE	Yes	input		73070.371208	43421.040999
VALUE	Yes	input		101949.83349	58210.603775
YOJ	No	input		8.7973097826	7.6384370166
YOJ_IYNC	Yes	input	log((YOJ + 1))	2.0870694656	0.7701217279

The name of the new variable is composed of some key letters from the original variable (YOJ) and some random alphanumeric characters (IYNC). Observe that the original variable has Keep=No while the newly created variable has Keep=Yes. This indicates that the original variable (YOJ) will no longer be available in any node that you place and connect after this Transform Variables node. Do not modify the values of Keep now.

The formula shows that Enterprise Miner has performed the log transformation after adding one to the value of YOJ. To understand why this has occurred, recall that YOJ has a minimum value of zero. The logarithm of zero is undefined, and the logarithm of something close to zero is extremely negative. Enterprise Miner takes this information into account and uses the transformation log(YOJ+1) to create a new variable that has values that are greater than or equal to zero (since the log(1)=0).

Inspect the distribution of the new variable, which is labeled log(YOJ).

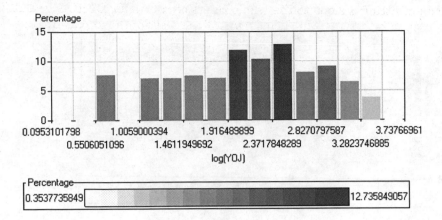

Now view the distribution of DEROG. The distribution of DEROG has a large proportion of observations at DEROG=0 and relatively few in which DEROG > 0.

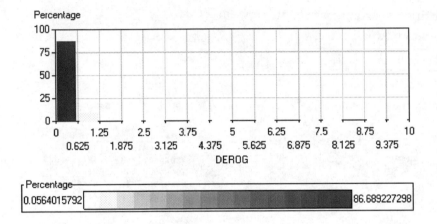

After viewing the distribution of DEROG, close the plot and view the distribution of DELINQ.

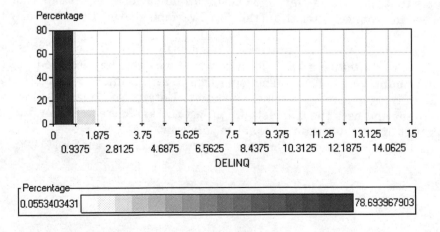

The same pattern that holds for DEROG also holds for DELINQ. In situations in which there is a large mass of points at one value and relatively few points spread out over the rest of the space, it is sometimes useful to group the levels of an interval variable.

Instead of fitting a slope to the whole range of values for DEROG or DELINQ, you need to estimate the mean in each group. Since most of the applicants in the data set had no delinquent credit lines, there is a high concentration of points at DELINQ=0. Close the plot when you are finished inspecting it.

Create a new variable INDEROG that indicates whether DEROG is greater than 0. Repeat the process for DELINQ but name the new variable INDELINQ.

To create the variable INDEROG:

1 Select

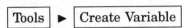

from the main menu. Alternately, you can click the Create Variable ( ) tool icon in the toolbox).

2 Type **INDEROG** in the Name box.

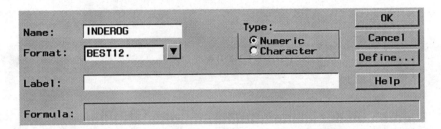

3 Select **Define**.

4 Type in the formula **DEROG > 0**.

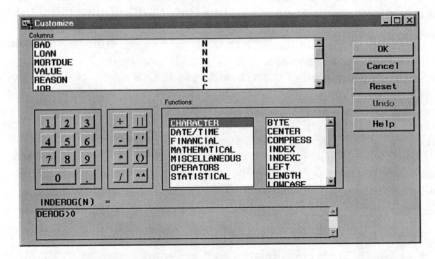

This definition is an example of Boolean logic and illustrates a way to dichotomize an interval variable. The statement is either true or false for each observation. When the statement is true, the expression evaluates as 1; otherwise, the expression evaluates as 0. In other words, when DEROG>0, INDEROG=1. Likewise, when DEROG=0, INDEROG=0. If the value of DEROG is missing, the expression evaluates as 0, since missing values are treated as being smaller than any nonmissing value in a numerical comparison. Since a missing value of DEROG is reasonably imputed as DEROG=0, this does not pose a problem for this example.

5 Select OK. Observe that the formula now appears in the Formula window.

Name:	INDEROG	Type:	OK
Format:	BEST12. ▼	⊙ Numeric	Cancel
		○ Character	Define...
Label:			Help
Formula:	DEROG>0		

6 Select ⟨OK⟩. The new variable, INDEROG, now appears in the list.

Name	Keep	Role	Formula	Mean	Std Dev	Skew
INDEROG	Yes	input	DEROG>0	0.118	0.3226888037	2.369976138

7 Repeat the steps for INDELINQ.

Name	Keep	Role	Formula	Mean	Std Dev
INDELINQ	Yes	input	DELINQ>0	0.1925	0.3943621568
INDEROG	Yes	input	DEROG>0	0.118	0.3226888037

Note that missing values of DELINQ result in INDELINQ=0 (see step 4 above). Since it is reasonable to impute DELINQ=0 when the value of DELINQ is missing, this does not pose a problem for this variable either.

Observe that even though DEROG and DELINQ were used to construct the new variables, the original variables are still available for analysis (Keep=Yes). You can modify this if you want. That is not done here since the created variables contain only a portion of the information that is contained in DEROG and DELINQ; specifically, they identify whether either DEROG or DELINQ is greater than zero.

Examine the distribution of NINQ. NINQ is a counting variable, but the majority of the observations have values of 0, 1, or 2. It may be useful to create a grouped version of NINQ by pooling all of the values larger than 2 (of which there are very few) into a new level 2+. This would create a new three-level grouping variable from NINQ. While creating a grouping variable that has three levels causes loss of information about the exact number of recent credit inquiries, it does enable you to handle nonlinearity in the relationship between NINQ and the response of interest.

First, create a new grouping variable that creates bins for the values of NINQ. You can create a grouping variable by using several different methods including the following:

☐ Bucket — creates cutoffs at approximately equally spaced intervals.

☐ Quantile — creates bins that have with approximately equal frequencies.

☐ Optimal Binning for Relationship to Target — creates cutoffs that yield an optimal relationship to the target (for binary targets).

The Optimal Binning for Relationship to Target transformation uses the DMSPLIT procedure to optimally split a variable into n groups with regard to a binary target. To create the n optimal groups, the procedure performs a recursive process of splitting the variable into groups that maximize the association with the target variable. The node uses the metadata to determine the optimum groups to speed processing. This binning transformation is useful when there is a nonlinear relationship between the input variable and a binary target. Enterprise Miner assigns an ordinal measurement level to the newly created variable. For more information, see the Transform Variables node in the Enterprise Miner Help.

Enterprise Miner provides help on a large number of topics in Help files that are organized for easy access. For example, to obtain software-based Help about binning transformations:

1 Select

The Contents tab should be active. If it is not, select Contents.

2 Scroll down the right panel of the window to the Transform Variables node.

3 Select **Transform Variables Node**.

4 Select **Creating Transformed variables**.

5 Select **Binning Transformations**.

Suppose you wanted to bin the values of NINQ into 0, 1, and 2+ (2 or more). To create the new binning variable:

1 Right-click the row for NINQ and select

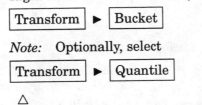

Note: Optionally, select

△

2 Change this number of buckets to 3 by using the arrows.

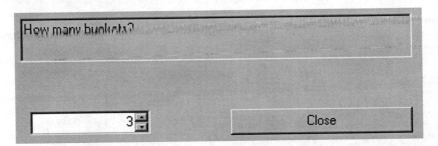

3 Select Close and inspect the plot that Enterprise Miner displays.

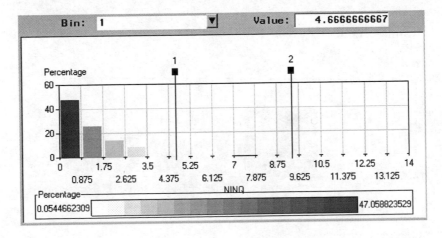

4 At the top of the window **Bin** is set to 1 by default. Type **0.5** in the **Value** box (for Bin 1) at the top of the window.

Note: Since NINQ is a counting variable, any value larger than zero and smaller than one would yield the same split that is provided by 0.5. △

5 Use the arrow next to **Bin** to change the selected bin from 1 to 2.

6 Type **1.5** in the **Value** box (for Bin 2). Inspect the resulting plot.

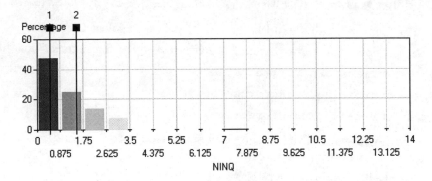

7 Close the chart to return to the Transform Variables window.

A new variable (NINQ_7RJ) is added to the table in this example. The new variable has the truncated name of the original variable that is followed by a random string of digits. Note that Enterprise Miner sets the value of **Keep** to **No** for the original variable. If you wanted to use both the binned variable and the original variable in the analysis, you would need to modify this attribute for NINQ and then set the value of **Keep** to **Yes**, but that is not done here. The descriptive statistics are based on metadata and your results, therefore, may vary slightly from those displayed here because of sampling variability.

Name	Keep	Role	Formula	Mean	Std Dev
YOJ	No	input		8.7973097826	7.6384370166
YOJ_IYNC	Yes	input	log((YOJ + 1))	2.0870694656	0.7701217279
DEROG	Yes	input		0.2413987592	0.8286221978
DELINQ	Yes	input		0.4532374101	1.2244732547
CLAGE	Yes	input		181.53016351	87.547191047
NINQ	No	input		1.148773842	1.6919826247
NINQ_7RJ	Yes	input	NINQ	1.148773842	1.6919826247
CLNO	Yes	input		21.125194805	10.23641608
DEBTINC	Yes	input		33.891762201	9.4603236863

Examine the distribution of the new variable.

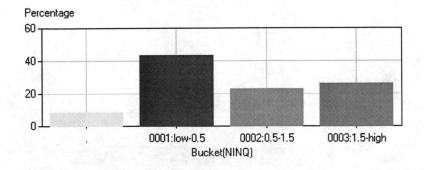

Observe that there are four histogram bars but only three bins. Observations that have a missing value for NINQ will also have a missing value for the binned version of NINQ. Inspect the other bins. The View Info tool reveals that over 40% of the data is in the second lowest category (NINQ=0), and over 20% is in the two top categories (NINQ=1 and NINQ>2), respectively. Almost 10% of the data has missing values for NINQ.

It might be appropriate at times to keep the original variable and the created variable. That is not done here. It is uncommon to keep both variables when the original variable and the transformed variable have the same measurement level (for example, when both variables are interval). Close the node when you are finished, saving changes when you are prompted.

Understanding Data Replacement

Add another Replacement node. Your new diagram should appear as follows:

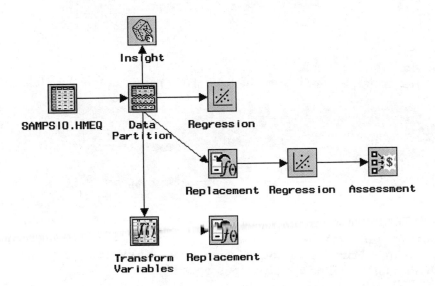

Open the newly added Replacement node. The Defaults tab is displayed first. Select the **Create imputed indicator variables** check box. The model role for these indicator variables is rejected. Later, you will specify input as the model role for some of the indicator variables, but do not do that now.

☑ Create imputed indicator variables:
New variable name prefix: M_
Role: rejected ▼
Indicator value: 1

This box requests the creation of new variables, each having a prefix M_, which have a value of 1 when an observation has a missing value for the associated variable and 0 otherwise. The regression and the neural network model can use these newly created indicator variables to identify observations that had missing values before the imputation.

The Replacement node enables you to replace certain values before imputing. For example, a data set may have all missing values coded as 999. In this case, you can check the box next to **Replace before imputation**; then replace the coded value by using the Constant values subtab on the Defaults tab. This is not shown here.

Using the Replacement Node

Select the Data tab of the Replacement node. To view the training data set, select **Training** and then select Properties. Information about the data set appears. Select **Table View** to see the data. The training data set is shown below. Deselect the **Variable labels** check box to see the variable names.

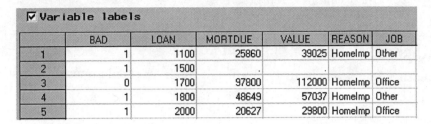

Close the Data Set Details window.
Select the Training subtab from the lower-right corner of the Data tab.

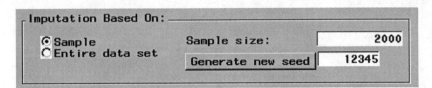

By default, the imputation is based on a random sample of the training data. The seed is used to initialize the randomization process. Generating a new seed creates a different sample. Now use the entire training data set by selecting **Entire data set**. The subtab information now appears as pictured below.

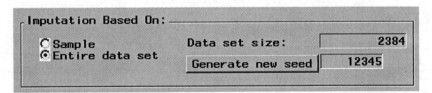

Return to the Defaults tab and select the Imputation Methods subtab. This shows that the default imputation method for Interval Variables is the **mean** (of the random sample from the training data set or of the entire training data set, depending on the settings in the Data tab). By default, imputation for Class Variables is done using the most frequently occurring level (or mode) in the same sample. If the most commonly occurring value is missing, Enterprise Miner uses the second most frequently occurring level in the sample.

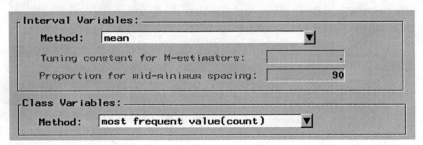

Click the arrow (▼) next to the method for interval variables. Enterprise Miner provides the following methods for imputing missing values for interval variables:

□ Mean (default) — the arithmetic average.

□ Median — the 50th percentile.

□ Midrange — the maximum plus the minimum divided by two.

□ Distribution-based — Replacement values are calculated based on the random percentiles of the variable's distribution.

□ Tree imputation — Replacement values are estimated by using a decision tree that uses the remaining input and rejected variables that have a status of **use** in the Tree Imputation tab.

□ Tree imputation with surrogates — the same as Tree imputation, but this method uses surrogate variables for splitting whenever a split variable has a missing values. In regular tree imputation, all observations that have a missing value for the split variable are placed in the same node. Surrogate splits use alternate (or surrogate) variables for splitting when the primary split variable is missing, so observations that have a missing value on the primary split variable are not necessarily placed in the same node. See the Tree node in the Enterprise Miner Help for more information about surrogates.

□ Mid-minimum spacing — In calculating this statistic, the data is trimmed by using N percent of the data as specified in the Proportion for mid-minimum spacing field. By default, the middle 90% of the data is used to trim the original data. The maximum plus the minimum divided by two for the trimmed distribution is equal to the mid-minimum spacing.

□ Tukey's biweight, Huber's, and Andrew's wave — These are robust M-estimators of location. This class of estimators minimizes functions of the deviations of the observations from the estimate that are more general than the sum of squared deviations or the sum of absolute deviations. M-estimators generalize the idea of the maximum-likelihood estimator of the location parameter in a specified distribution.

□ Default constant — You can set a default value to be imputed for some or all variables. Instructions for using this method appear later in this section.

□ None — turns off the imputation for the interval variables.

Click the ▼ next to the method for class variables. Enterprise Miner provides several of the same methods for imputing missing values for class variables including distribution-based, tree imputation, tree imputation with surrogates, default constant, and none. You can also select the most frequent value (count) that uses the mode of the data that is used for imputation. If the most commonly occurring value for a variable is missing, Enterprise Miner uses the next most frequently occurring value.

Select **Tree imputation** as the imputation method for both types of variables.

```
┌─Interval Variables:───────────────────────────────────
│  Method:       │tree imputation              ▼│
│
│  Tuning constant for M-estimators:    │              .│
│  Proportion for mid-minimum spacing:  │           90 │
│
┌─Class Variables:──────────────────────────────────────
│  Method:       │tree imputation              ▼│
```

This tab sets the default imputation method for each type of variable. You will later see how to change the imputation method for a variable. When you are using tree imputation for imputing missing values, use the entire training data set for more consistent results.

Select the Constant Values subtab of the Defaults tab. This subtab enables you to replace certain values (before imputing, if you want, by using the check box on the General subtab of the Defaults tab). It also enables you to specify constants for imputing missing values. Type **0** in the imputation box for numeric variables and **Unknown** in the imputation box for character variables.

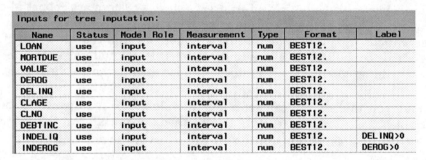

The constants that are specified in this tab are used to impute the missing values for a variable when you select **default constant** as the imputation method. This example uses tree imputation as the default imputation method; however, a later example modifies the imputation method for some of the variables to use the default constant that is specified here.

Select the Tree Imputation tab. This tab enables you to set the variables that will be used for tree imputation.

Inputs for tree imputation:

Name	Status	Model Role	Measurement	Type	Format	Label
LOAN	use	input	interval	num	BEST12.	
MORTDUE	use	input	interval	num	BEST12.	
VALUE	use	input	interval	num	BEST12.	
DEROG	use	input	interval	num	BEST12.	
DELINQ	use	input	interval	num	BEST12.	
CLAGE	use	input	interval	num	BEST12.	
CLNO	use	input	interval	num	BEST12.	
DEBTINC	use	input	interval	num	BEST12.	
INDELIQ	use	input	interval	num	BEST12.	DELINQ>0
INDEROG	use	input	interval	num	BEST12.	DEROG>0

Note that the target variable (BAD) is not available, and rejected variables have Status set to **don't use** by default. To use a rejected variable, you can set the Status to **use** by right-clicking the row of the variable and then selecting

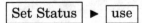

However, none of the variables in the data set have been rejected, so this is not a consideration for this example.

Select the Interval Variables tab.

Name	Status	Model Role	Imputation Method
LOAN	use	input	tree imputation
MORTDUE	use	input	tree imputation
VALUE	use	input	tree imputation
DEROG	use	input	tree imputation
DELINQ	use	input	tree imputation
CLAGE	use	input	tree imputation
CLNO	use	input	tree imputation
DEBTINC	use	input	tree imputation
INDELIQ	use	input	tree imputation
INDEROG	use	input	tree imputation
YOJ_IYNC	use	input	tree imputation

Suppose you want to change the imputation method for VALUE to **mean**. To do so, right-click in the **Imputation Method** column for VALUE and select

Select Method ▶ Mean

Suppose you want to change the imputed value for DEROG and DELINQ to zero. Although zero is the default constant, you can practice setting up this imputed value by using different methods. Use **Default Constant** to impute the values for DEROG, but use **Set Value** to specify the imputed value for DELINQ. To change the imputation method for DEROG, right-click in the **Imputation Method** column for DEROG and select

Select Method ▶ default constant

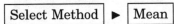

Now set the imputation method for DELINQ.

1 Right-click in the **Imputation Method** column for DELINQ.

2 Select

Select Method ▶ Set Value

3 Type **0** in the **New Value** box.

4 Select OK.

A portion of the window is shown below.

Name	Status	Model Role	Imputation Method
LOAN	use	input	tree imputation
MORTDUE	use	input	tree imputation
VALUE	use	input	mean
DEROG	use	input	default constant - 0
DELINQ	use	input	set value - 0
CLAGE	use	input	tree imputation
CLNO	use	input	tree imputation
DEBTINC	use	input	tree imputation
INDELIQ	use	input	tree imputation
INDEROG	use	input	tree imputation
YOJ_IYNC	use	input	tree imputation

Even though you specified the imputation in different ways, the imputed value for DEROG and DELINQ will be the same. Were you to change the default constant value, however, it would affect the imputation for DEROG but not for DELINQ.

Select the Class Variables tab. Observe that the Status of BAD is set to **don't use**, which indicates that the missing values for this variable will not be replaced.

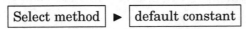

Name	Status	Imputation Method	Replace Value
BAD	don't use	tree imputation	
REASON	use	tree imputation	
JOB	use	tree imputation	
NINQ_7RJ	use	tree imputation	

Suppose that you want to use **Unknown** (the default constant) as the imputed value for REASON, and you want to use **Other** as the imputed value for JOB. To modify the imputation method for REASON

1 Right-click in the **Imputation Method** column of the row for REASON:

2 Select

$\boxed{\text{Select method}}$ ▶ $\boxed{\text{default constant}}$

To modify the imputation method for JOB:

1 Right-click in the **Imputation Method** column of the row for JOB.

2 Select

$\boxed{\text{Select method}}$ ▶ $\boxed{\text{set value}}$

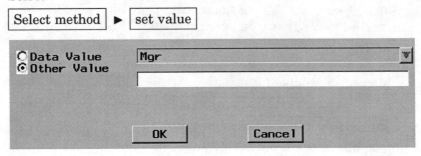

3 Select **Data Value**.

4 Use the 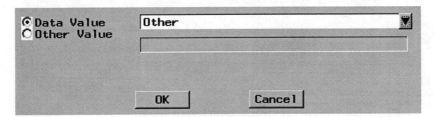 to select **Other** from the list of data values.

5 Select $\boxed{\text{OK}}$.

Inspect the resulting window. Your settings should match those shown below.

Name	Status	Imputation Method
BAD	don't use	tree imputation
REASON	use	default constant - Unknown
JOB	use	set value - Other
NINQ_7RJ	use	tree imputation

Select the Output tab. While the Data tab shows the input data, the Output tab shows the output data set information.

```
Show details of:
 ⊙ Training      ○ Validation     ○ Test        ○ Score

 Library: EMDATA      Data set: RTRNQPH1    [ Properties... ]
 Description:    [Data Replacement Train            ]
```

Close the Replacement node and save the changes when you are prompted.
The Replacement node will be used as inputs for modeling nodes in later sections.

Understanding Interactive Grouping

An alternative way to process the data before modeling is to use the Interactive
Grouping node in Enterprise Miner Release 4.2. The Interactive Grouping node enables
you to automatically group variable values into classes based on the node settings, and
to optionally modify the initially generated classes (groups) interactively. By using the
node, you can manage the number of groups of a variable, improve the predictive power
of a variable, select predictive variables, generate the Weight of Evidence (WOE) for
each group of a variable, and make the WOE vary smoothly or even linearly across the
groups.

The WOE for a group is defined as the logarithm of the ratio of the proportion of
nonevent observations in the group over the proportion of event observations in the
group. For the binary target variable BAD in this example, BAD=1 (a client who
defaulted on a loan) is the event level and BAD=0 (a client who repaid a loan) is the
nonevent level. WOE measures the relative risk of a group. Therefore, high negative
values of WOE correspond to high risk of loan default; high positive values correspond
to low risk.

After the grouping of variable values has been defined for a variable, you can assess
the predictive power of the variable. The predictive power of a variable is the ability of
the variable to distinguish event and nonevent observations. In this example, it is the
ability to separate bad loan clients from good loan clients. You can assess the predictive
power by using one the following criteria:

- □ Information Value — is the weighted sum of WOE over the groups. The weight is
  the difference between the proportion of nonevents and the proportion of events in
  each group.

- □ Gini Score — is the same as the Gini index in the Tree node. See the Interactive
  Grouping node in the Enterprise Miner Help for more information.

The WOE variables are usually used as inputs in successor modeling nodes.

Performing Interactive Grouping

Add an Interactive Grouping node and connect it to the Data Partition node as
shown below.

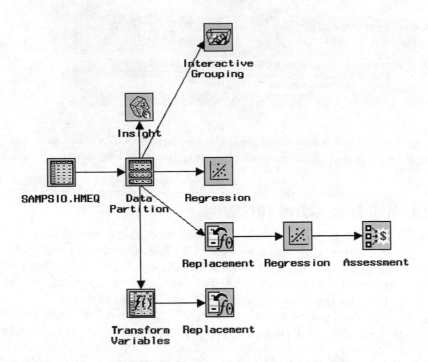

Open the Interactive Grouping node. The Variables tab is displayed first. Select from the main menu

to open the IGN Settings window.

The IGN Settings window enables you to specify the settings that the node uses to perform automatic grouping. The Interactive Grouping node enables you apply the Information Value or Gini Score criteria to variables for evaluating their predictive power. In this case, you can select the **Auto-Commit** check box. In addition, you can export the grouping statistics to a SAS data set by selecting the **Export Grouping Statistics on Commit** check box and specifying a valid SAS data set name in the **Dataset** box.

The **Freeze Node** check box enables you to prevent the user-modified grouping from being overwritten by the automatic grouping results when you run the node.

In this example, select the **Auto-Commit** check box, select **Information Value** as the commit criterion, and change the commit value to 0.3. Also, select the **Export Grouping Statistics on Commit** check box.

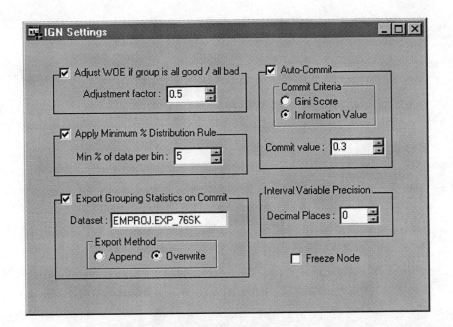

Close the IGN Settings window and run the node. The Interactive Grouping uses the settings to perform automatic grouping. In automatic grouping, the grouping of a variable is committed when its Information Value or Gini Score is greater than the commit value that you specify in the node settings.

After the node run is complete, click Yes when a window prompts you to view the results. The Output tab of the Results window lists the Keep status, Commit Type, and the values of Information Value and Gini Score. Notice that the Keep status of the variables that have Information Value less than 0.3 is set to **NO**.

Interactive Grouping Output Summary

Variable	Keep	Commit Type	Auto-Grouped Infoval	Committed Infoval	Auto-Grouped Gini	Committed Gini
CLAGE	YES	AUTO	0.32282	0.32282	31.4832	31.4832
CLNO	NO		0.13905	.	20.7734	.
DEBTINC	YES	AUTO	1.93230	1.93230	67.2157	67.2157
DELINQ	YES	AUTO	0.58000	0.58000	33.4093	33.4093
DEROG	YES	AUTO	0.36493	0.36493	22.3987	22.3987
JOB	NO		0.10552	.	16.9370	.
LOAN	NO		0.23764	.	23.9369	.
MORTDUE	NO		0.21016	.	24.2786	.
NINQ	NO		0.21576	.	23.5221	.
REASON	NO		0.01490	.	5.9006	.
VALUE	YES	AUTO	0.74527	0.74527	38.2942	38.2942
YOJ	NO		0.10181	.	17.1020	.

Close the Results window and close the node.

To modify the results of automatic grouping, right-click the Interactive Grouping node in your Diagram Workspace and select **Interactive**.

The following display shows the Chart tab.

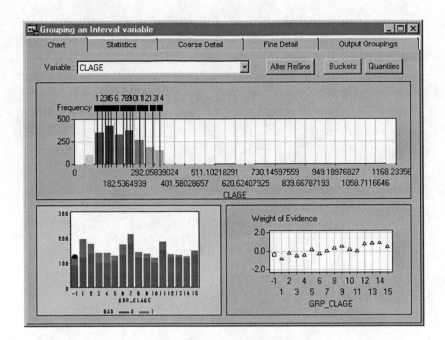

Select the ▼ next to **Variables** to specify the variable CLAGE. The Chart tab displays several charts for CLAGE:

- □ a distribution histogram for CLAGE that is overlayed by the reference lines that define the grouping.
- □ a vertical stacked bar chart that shows the proportion of defaulters (1's) and non-defaulters (0's) for each group.
- □ a line plot of the WOE values for each group.

Observe that the WOE line plot displays a group that is numbered as -1, which means that the group is formed by missing values in the variable. You can manually join this group to the other group. However, any subsequent changes to the groups will assign the missing values to their own distinct group again.

There is no single criterion to obtain satifactory grouping for a variable. A linear or at least monotone increase or decrease of the WOE curve is often a better solution.

Select the Output Groupings tab. It displays the same information as the Output tab in the Results window. The variables CLAGE, DEBTINC, DELINQ, DEROG, and VALUE have a keep status of **Yes**.

Keep	Commit Type	Auto-Grouped Infoval	Committed Infoval	Auto-Grouped Gini	Committed Gini	Variable
YES	AUTO	0.32282	0.32282	31.48315	31.48315	CLAGE
NO		0.13905	.	20.77339	.	CLNO
YES	AUTO	1.9323	1.9323	67.21572	67.21572	DEBTINC
YES	AUTO	0.58	0.58	33.40933	33.40933	DELINQ
YES	AUTO	0.36493	0.36493	22.39867	22.39867	DEROG
NO		0.10552	.	16.93698	.	JOB
NO		0.23764	.	23.9369	.	LOAN
NO		0.21016	.	24.27859	.	MORTDUE
NO		0.21576	.	23.52207	.	NINQ
NO		0.0149	.	5.90057	.	REASON
YES	AUTO	0.74527	0.74527	38.29417	38.29417	VALUE
NO		0.10181	.	17.10195	.	YOJ

In order to reproduce the results that are displayed in this book, change the grouping as follows:

1 In the Chart tab, select the variable DEBTINC. Click [Alter Refline] and select **12**.

2 The Update Reference Line window opens.

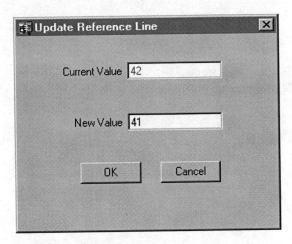

Type **41** in the **New Value** box and click [OK].

3 Select the Statistics tab, click [Commit Grouping]. Then, select the Output Groupings tab. Observe that the Commit Type for the variable DEBTINC has been changed from **AUTO** to **USER**.

4 Go back to the Chart tab and select the variable NINQ.

5 Select the Coarse Detail tab. Select the row for group 4 and right-click. Select [Merge] ► [5]

6 Select the Statistics tab, click [Commit Grouping]. Select the Output Groupings tab again and observe that the Keep status for NINQ is set to **Yes** and the Commit Type is **USER**.

Keep	Commit Type	Auto-Grouped Infoval	Committed Infoval	Auto-Grouped Gini	Committed Gini	Variable
YES	AUTO	0.32282	0.32282	31.48315	31.48315	CLAGE
NO		0.13905	.	20.77339	.	CLNO
YES	USER	1.9323	1.88917	67.21572	66.88724	DEBTINC
YES	AUTO	0.58	0.58	33.40933	33.40933	DELINQ
YES	AUTO	0.36493	0.36493	22.39867	22.39867	DEROG
NO		0.10552	.	16.93698		JOB
NO		0.23764	.	23.9369	.	LOAN
NO		0.21016	.	24.27859	.	MORTDUE
YES	USER	0.21576	0.17554	23.52207	22.72475	NINQ
NO		0.0149	.	5.90057	.	REASON
YES	AUTO	0.74527	0.74527	38.29417	38.29417	VALUE
NO		0.10181	.	17.10195		YOJ

7 Close the Grouping an Interval Variable window. Click [Yes] when you are prompted to freeze the node.

When a grouping is committed for a variable, the Interactive Grouping node generates the following variables:

☐ LBL_<*variable-name*> — the label of the group.

☐ GRP_<*variable-name*> — the group identification number.

☐ WOE_<*variable-name*> — the WOE value.

The WOE variables will be used as inputs for creating a model in the following section.

Fitting and Comparing Candidate Models

Fitting a Regression Model

Add a new Regression node and connect it to the recently modified Replacement node. Then connect the Regression node to the Assessment node. Compare your flow to the one below.

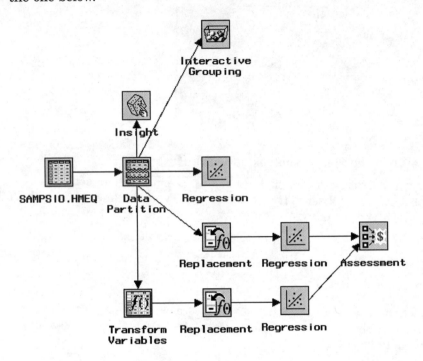

Open the Regression node that you just added to the workspace. From the main menu, select

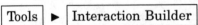

The Interaction Builder enables you to easily add interactions and higher order terms to the model, although that is not shown now. A portion of this tool is shown below.

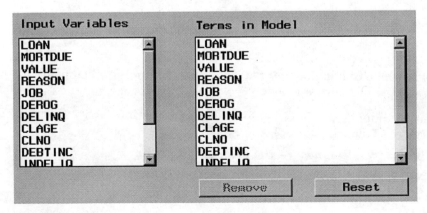

The input variables are shown on the left, while the effects in the model are shown on the right. The Regression node fits a model that contains all main effects by default. Close the Interaction Builder window without making any changes.

Select the Selection Method tab. This tab enables you to perform different types of variable selection by using various criteria. No variable selection is done by default.

You can choose from the following variable selection techniques:

□ Backward — begins, by default, with all candidate effects in the model and then systematically removes effects that are not significantly associated with the target until no other effect in the model meets the Stay Significance Level, or until the Stop criterion is met. This method is not recommended for binary or ordinal targets when there are many candidate effects or when there are many levels for some classification input variables.

□ Forward — begins, by default, with no candidate effects in the model and then systematically adds effects that are significantly associated with the target until none of the remaining effects meet the Entry Significance Level or until the Stop criterion is met.

□ Stepwise — As in the Forward method, Stepwise selection begins, by default, with no candidate effects in the model and then systematically adds effects that are significantly associated with the target. However, after an effect is added to the model, Stepwise may remove any effect that is already in the model, but that is not significantly associated with the target.

□ None — (default) all candidate effects are included in the final model.

Select Stepwise by using the ▼ next to the **Method** box.

Method:	Stepwise ▼
Criteria:	Profit / Loss ▼

Inspect the **Effect Hierarchy** options in the lower-left corner of the General subtab of the Selection Method tab.

Effect Hierarchy
- ☐ Sequential
- Variable type: Class ▼
- Moving effect rule: None ▼

Model hierarchy refers to the requirement that for any effect in the model, all effects that it contains must also be in the model. For example, in order for the interaction A*B to be in the model, the main effects A and B must also be in the model. The **Effect Hierarchy** options enable you to control how a set of effects is entered into or removed from the model during the effect-selection process. No changes are necessary for the purposes of this example.

Select the Criteria subtab.

☑ Defaults:

Number of variables:

Start: 0   Stop: 14   Significance Levels:

Force: 0   Entry: 0.05

                                Stay: 0.05

Stepwise stopping criteria: 28

Consider the choices under **Number of Variables** in the lower-right corner of the window. The items here enable you to select a specified number of effects to begin the selection process (for forward) or select a minimum number of effects to remain in the model. The order depends on the order that is displayed in the Interaction Builder. To change the order of effects, you can select

Tools ▶ Model Ordering

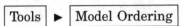

but no ordering is done for this example.

Stepwise Stopping Criteria enables you to set the maximum number of steps before the Stepwise method stops. The default is set to twice the number of effects in the model. **Stop** enables you to set the maximum (for Forward method) or minimum (for Backward method) number of effects to be included in the model.

The Stepwise method uses cutoffs for variables to enter the model and for variables to leave the model. Changing these values might affect the final variables that are included in the model. In this example, clear the selection of the **Defaults** check box, change the value of **Stepwise Stopping Criteria** to **14**, and change the value of **Stay Significant Level** to **0.025**.

Close the Regression node and save the changes when you are prompted. Since you have changed the default settings for the node, you will be prompted to change the default model name. Type **StepReg** for the model name.

Model Name: StepReg

Model Description:

        OK   Cancel

Select OK.

Evaluating the Model

Right-click the Assessment node and select **Run**. This enables you to generate and compare lift charts for the two regression models. Observe that each node becomes green as it runs. Since you ran the flow from the Assessment node, you are prompted to see the Assessment results. Select Yes to see these results. Inspect the table that appears. If you scroll the window to the right, Enterprise Miner displays several typical regression statistics such as asymptotic standard error (ASE).

Tool	Name	Description	Target	Target Event
Regression	Untitled	Regression	BAD	1
Regression	StepReg	Regression	BAD	1

Since more than one Regression node is connected to the Assessment node, you need to use the model name to identify which regression came from the default regression model and which one came from the stepwise regression model. Observe that one line has the name StepReg, but the other line has the name Untitled. Rename the model that is currently named Untitled to DefReg since it represents the default regression model that uses the default data imputation. Press the ENTER key to enter the new name before you proceed. Highlight both rows to select them and then select

| Tools | ▶ | Lift Chart |

A cumulative %Response chart is shown by default. You can see which line belongs to which model by selecting

| Format | ▶ | Model Name |

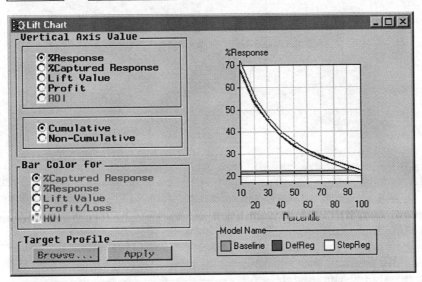

Recall that this chart groups individuals based on the predicted probability of response, and then plots the percentage of respondents. The two lines are almost indistinguishable in this case.

Recall that the DefReg model was created with the effect selection method set to **none**. That is, all candidate effects are included in the final model. You might want to know what variables are included in the StepReg model. Close the Lift Chart window to return to the Assessment Tool window. Highlight the row for the StepReg model in the table to select it and then select from the main menu of a opened Assessment node

| View | ▶ | Model Results |

The Output tab of the Regression Results window displays the SAS output at each step of the stepwise logistic regression analysis. The model construction stops at step 13 when the Wald Chi-Square test criterion removes the last effect (variable) VALUE that you entered into the model. The stepwise regression model includes all variables except VALUE and MORTDUE.

Fitting a Default Decision Tree

Add a default Tree node, connect the Data Partition node to the Tree node, and then connect the Tree node to the Assessment node. The flow should now appear like the following flow.

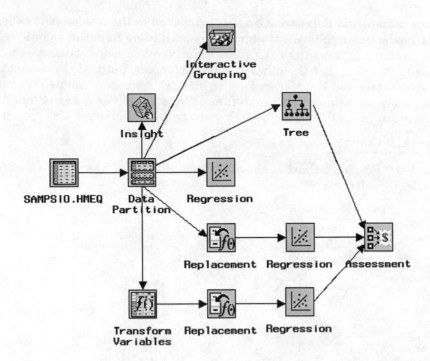

You might want to know why the tree is connected to the Data Partition node and not to the Replacement node. The reason is that a decision tree handles missing values directly, so it does not need data replacement. Monotonic transformations of interval numeric variables will probably not improve the tree fit since the tree groups numeric variables into bins. In fact, the tree may actually perform worse if you connect it after you group a variable into bins in the Transform Variables node. The bins reduce the splits that the tree can consider unless you include the original variable and the grouped variable in the model.

Run the flow from the Assessment node and select ⬜Yes when you are prompted to view the results. Nodes that have been executed previously are not run again. The Assessment node opens and displays three models.

Type the name **DefTree** in the **Name** column for the Tree tool to indicate that you have fit a default tree. Your window should now look like the one below.

Tool	Name	Description	Target	Target Event
Tree	DefTree	Tree	BAD	1
Regression	DefReg	Regression	BAD	1
Regression	StepReg	Regression	BAD	1

Your models might appear in different order depending on the sequence in which you connected and ran each of the nodes. The **Description** column also contains different values. The **Description** is used by Enterprise Miner to distinguish among the models. None of these potential naming or order differences has any impact on the results.

To generate a lift chart, highlight all rows in the Assessment node to select them. You can do this by selecting the row for one model and then CTRL-clicking on the rows for the other models. You can also drag through all of the rows to select them simultaneously.

The lift chart that you will construct is based on the validation data set. To verify that the validation data set is being used, inspect the **Tools** menu and observe the check mark next to **Validation Data Set**. Enterprise Miner does not compute assessment information for all data sets by default, so not all charts are available on all data sets. From the main menu, select

You can now compare how the models perform on the validation data set. Observe that the tree model outperforms both regression models.

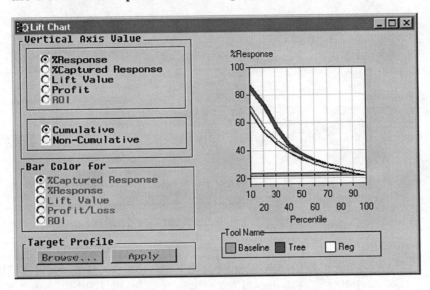

Occasionally the entire legend is not visible. You can often see the entire legend by maximizing the window. Otherwise, it may be necessary to modify the graph window. To modify the graph window,

1 Click the Move/Resize Legend icon ( ) on the toolbox at the top to move or resize the legend. Click a side of the legend box to resize (the cursor appears as a double-sided arrow). Click in the middle to move the legend (the cursor appears as a hand). Dragging resizes or moves the legend, depending on the cursor appearance.

The resized legend appears below.

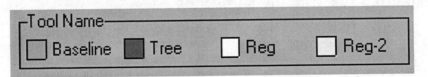

2 Click the Move Graph icon ( ) on the toolbox and reposition the graph. The default legend and formatted legend are pictured below. To use the names that you typed, select from the Enterprise Miner main menu at the top of the window

Inspect the plot and observe that the default tree seems to greatly outperform both of the regression models.

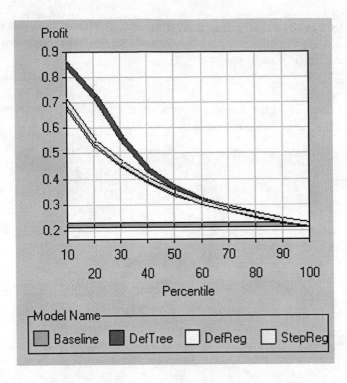

One possible reason for the difference could lie in the fact that decision trees are highly flexible modeling techniques. Regression models, by comparison, are relatively inflexible unless you add additional terms such as interactions or polynomial effects. Another reason could be the way in which decision trees handle missing values. Recall that you had to impute missing values before building a regression model on all of the training data, while decision trees can handle missing values without imputation.

To evaluate the extent of the difference that may be attributable to the inflexibility of the regression model, consider fitting a neural network model. Although neural networks require complete observations (just like regression models), they are extremely flexible. Close the Assessment node when you have finished inspecting the various lift charts.

Exploring the Tree Model Results

The Tree Desktop Application is a Microsoft Windows application that displays tables and graphs in separate windows. These windows may be independently arranged or hidden. The graphs are easily printed and copied with good presentation quality.

Note: The application was called Tree Results Viewer in Enterprise Miner Releases 4.0 and 4.1 △

The Tree Desktop Application in Enterprise Miner, Release 4.2 functions in two modes: viewer mode and SAS mode. The SAS mode enables you to view the model results and to construct your decision tree model in an automatic and an interactive modes. The viewer mode is discussed in this section.

To launch the Tree Desktop Application in view mode from Enterprise Miner, right-click a Tree node and select **Tree Viewer**.

Note: SAS mode is experimental for EM4.2. △

The Tree Desktop Application contains 15 tables and graphs. When you launch the Tree Desktop Application, it displays four views by default, as shown below.

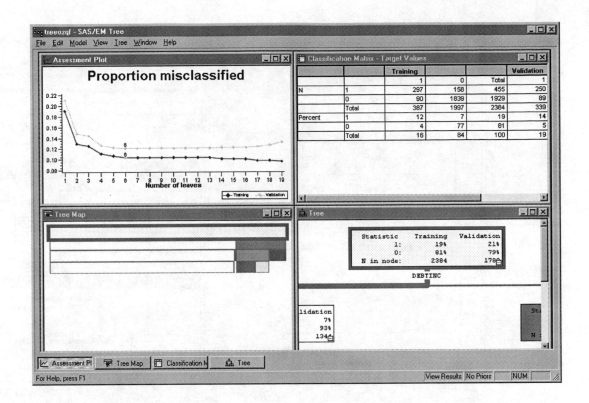

Use the **View** main menu to select a view to open. For this example, select

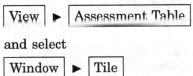

| View | ▶ | Assessment Table |

and select

| Window | ▶ | Tile |

Tile arranges the views as shown in the following displays. The following display shows several views, including Assessment Table, Assessment Plot, Tree Map, Classification Matrix, and Tree.

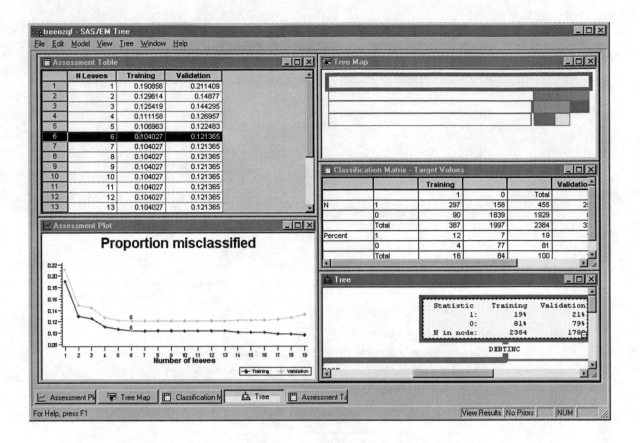

The assessment table and assessment plot display the training and validation (if available) assessment values for several candidate subtrees. These views reveal how large a tree is needed for a sufficient fit, and whether the problem of overfitting is present in large trees. If the classification for the training and validation data are similar across all subtrees, no overfitting is present in the training data. By default, the subtree with the highest assessment values for validation and the fewest number of leaves is selected. In this example, the target variable BAD is binary. By default, the misclassification rate is used as the model assessment measure for a binary target. The subtrees that have six to thirteen leaves have the smallest value of misclassification rates (0.121365) for validation. Therefore, the subtree with six leaves is selected.

The classification matrix summarizes the prediction for each level of the categorial target variable. For the selected six-leaf tree, 12% of the defaulters (1s) are classified correctly in the training data. Of the nondefaulters (0s), 77% are classified correctly in the training data. For the validation data, 14% of the defaulters and 74% of the nondefaulters are correctly classified.

The tree displays node statistics, splitting variables, and splitting rules. The top node represents the entire training data set. By default, the node color is proportional to the percentage of defaulters. The line width is proportional to the ratio of the number of training observations in a branch to the number of training observations in the root node. The line color is constant. You can change the node color, line color, and width by right-clicking within the tree view and selecting **Tree View Properties**. To change the display of the node statistics and splitting rules, right-click within the tree view and select **Node Statistics**. In this example, the first split is based on the values of the variable DEBTINC.

The tree map is a compact representation of the whole tree. The width of a node in the tree map represents node size. The nodes are colored in the same manner as the tree view.

For more information, see the Help for the Enterprise Miner Tree Desktop Application by selecting from the main menu

| Help | ▶ | Help Topics |

or by pressing the F1 key when the application is launched.

Fitting a Default Neural Network

Add a default Neural Network node. Connect the most recently added Replacement node to the Neural Network, and then connect the Neural Network node to the Assessment node. The flow should now appear like the one below.

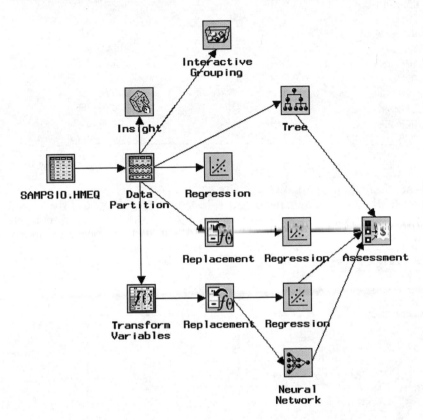

Note: The SAS Process Monitor appears when the neural network is executed. This monitor enables you to stop the neural network at any time. If the monitor does not show any activity for a few moments, select Stop and then Continue on the monitor to restart the process. The monitor may not appear when you run in client/server mode, depending on your machine settings. △

Run the flow from the Neural Network node. Select Yes when you are prompted to view the results. The default Neural Network node fits a multilayer perceptron (MLP) model with no direct connections, and the number of hidden layers is data dependent. In this example, the Neural Network node fitted a MLP model with a single hidden layer.

By default, the Tables tab in the Neural Network Results Browser displays various statistics of the fitted model.

Click the Weights tab. The Weights tab displays the weights (parameter estimates) of the connections. The following display shows the weights of the connections from each variable to the single hidden layer. Each level of each class variable is also connected to the hidden layer. The Neural Network node iteratively adjusts the weights of the connections to minimize the error function. Note that your results may vary from those that are displayed below.

	From	To	Weight
1	CLAGE	H11	0.2487032744
2	CLNO	H11	0.0491284652
3	DEBTINC	H11	-0.211814517
4	DELINQ	H11	-0.255474436
5	DEROG	H11	-0.055095013
6	INDELINQ	H11	-0.077200117
7	INDEROG	H11	-0.101200356
8	LOAN	H11	0.0880216206
9	MORTDUE	H11	0.140058316
10	VALUE	H11	-0.147674847
11	YOJ_7UYL	H11	0.1335157062
12	JOBMgr	H11	-0.111290423
13	JOBOffice	H11	0.2639321581
14	JOBOther	H11	0.0024737952
15	JOBProfExe	H11	0.0704215546
16	JOBSales	H11	-0.219647973

Close the Neural Network Results Browser.

Right-click the Assessment node and select **Results**. Rename the neural network from Untitled to DefNN. To compare model results, highlight all four models to select them and then select

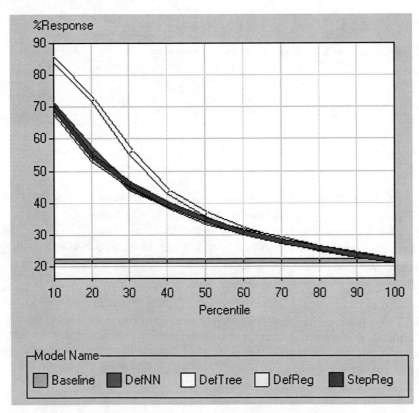

Investigating the Regression and Neural Network Models

The default neural network does not perform any better than the regression model. If both models perform poorly compared to the decision tree, poor performance may be due to how missing values are handled. The tree will handle observations that have missing values, while the regression and neural network models will ignore observations that have missing values.

To handle the missing values, you added an imputation node so that all of the observations would be used for building and evaluating the model. The effect of this replacement, however, is that you replace a missing value (perhaps an unusual value for the variable) with an imputed value (a typical value for the variable). Imputation can therefore change an observation from being somewhat unusual with respect to a particular variable to very typical with respect to that variable. For example, if someone were applying for a loan and had a missing value for INCOME, the Replacement node (by default) would replace that value with the mean for INCOME in a sample from the training data. In practice, someone who has an average value for INCOME would often be evaluated differently from someone who has a missing value for INCOME on a loan application; however, the regression and neural network models could not distinguish between these two cases.

One solution to this problem is to create missing value indicators to indicate if an observation originally had a missing value before imputation was performed. The missing value indicators allow the regression and neural network models to differentiate between observations that originally had missing values and those observations that have nonmissing values. The addition of missing value indicators can greatly improve a neural network or regression model.

Recall that you checked the box to add these indicators in the last Replacement node. To find out what happened to these indicators, open the most recently edited Regression node. The Variables tab is active. Scroll to the bottom of the tab. A portion of the output is shown below.

Name	Status	Model Role	Measurement
M_CLNO	don't use	rejected	binary
M_DEBTIN	don't use	rejected	binary
M_INDELI	don't use	rejected	unary
M_INDERO	don't use	rejected	unary
M_YOJ_IY	don't use	rejected	binary
M_REASON	don't use	rejected	binary
M_JOB	don't use	rejected	binary
M_NINQ_7	don't use	rejected	binary

Specify the indicators that you want to consider in your model by setting their status to **use**. Those missing value indicators whose measurement level is unary have only one level. The presence of one level implies that the corresponding variable has no missing values (or all missing values). Therefore, these missing value indicators will not be useful in the model.

Previous investigation has determined that a missing value for DEBTINC is strongly related to the target; therefore, change the status of M_DEBTIN (the missing value indicator for DEBTINC) to **use** and rerun the regression model.

Name	Status	Model Role	Measurement
M_CLNO	don't use	rejected	binary
M_DEBTIN	use	rejected	binary
M_INDELI	don't use	rejected	unary

Close the Regression node, saving changes when you are prompted. Rerun the flow from the Assessment node, and view the results when you are prompted. Build a lift chart for the decision tree (DefTree) and the new regression model (StepReg). Investigate whether adding the missing value indicator variable has made a difference.

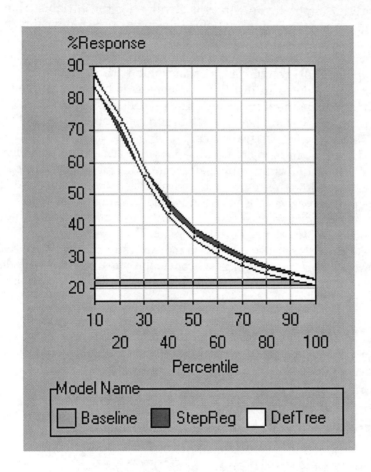

Now the regression model outperforms the tree in the first decile. Both models have very similar performance on the validation data set. This example illustrates that missing variables can have a dramatic impact on performance.

Fitting a Regression Model

Add a Regression node, connect the Interactive Grouping node to the Regression node, and then connect the Regression node to the Assessment node. The diagram should now appears as follows:

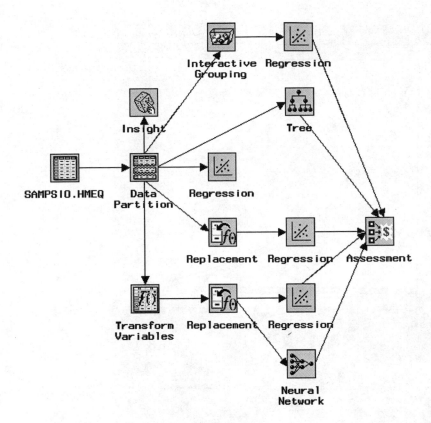

Open the Regression node. The Variables tab is active by default. Change the status of all input variables except the WOE_ variables to **don't use**.

Name	Status	Model Role	Measurement	Type	Format
WOE_VALUE	use	input	interval	num	BEST12.
WOE_NINQ	use	input	interval	num	BEST12.
WOE_DEROG	use	input	interval	num	BEST12.
WOE_DELINQ	use	input	interval	num	BEST12.
WOE_DEBTINC	use	input	interval	num	BEST12.
WOE_CLAGE	use	input	interval	num	BEST12.
BAD	use	target	binary	num	BEST12.
YOJ	don't use	input	interval	num	BEST12.

Close the Regression node and save the model. Name the model NewReg.

Run the flow from the Assessment node and select Yes when you are prompted to view the results. Create a lift chart for the stepwise regression model (StepReg) and the most recent regression model (NewReg). Investigate whether the incorporation of the Interactive Grouping node makes a difference. Both regression models have almost identical performance on the validation data set.

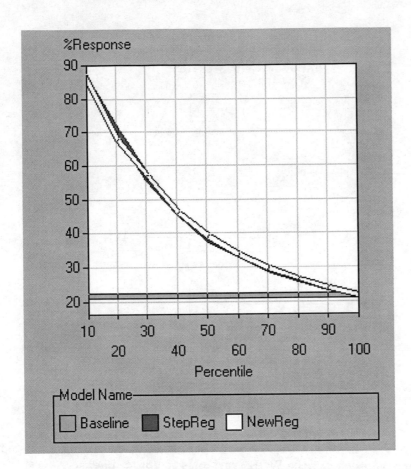

In general, it is impossible to know whether a decision tree, a regression model, or a neural network model will provide the best results. For this data (or for any other), a good analyst will consider many variations of each model and identify the best one according to his or her criteria. In this case, assume that the regression model (StepReg) is selected.

Generating and Using Scoring Code

After deciding on a model, you will often need to use your model to score new or existing observations. The Score node can be used to evaluate, save, and combine scoring code from different models. In this example, you want to score a data set by using the regression model.

Modify your workspace to appear like the diagram below as follows:

1 Drag a Score node onto the workspace and position it below the Assessment node.

2 Connect the Regression node to the Score node.

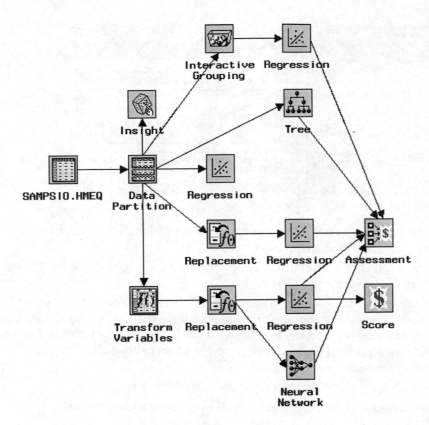

Open the Score node. The Settings tab is active. The Settings tab provides options for you when you run the Score node in a path. Part of the Settings tab is shown here.

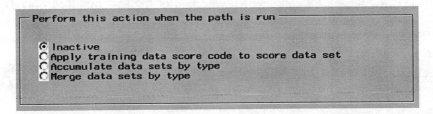

By default, no action is taken. The Score node collects scoring code, but it does not modify any data sets unless you change the settings on this tab. Do not change the settings now.

The following choices are available:

1 **Inactive** (default) — exports the most recently created scored data sets.

2 **Apply training data score code to score data set** — applies scoring code to the score data set.

3 **Accumulate data sets by type** — copies and exports data sets that are imported from predecessor nodes. If you use this action in a path that contains a group processing node, the output data sets are concatenated.

4 **Merge data sets by type** — merges data sets that are imported from predecessor nodes. For example, you can use this action to merge the training data sets from two modeling nodes to compare the predicted values.

The Score Code tab enables you to see the scoring code for each modeling node that is connected to the Score node. Only the Regression node is connected to the Score node, so you see only scoring code for the regression model.

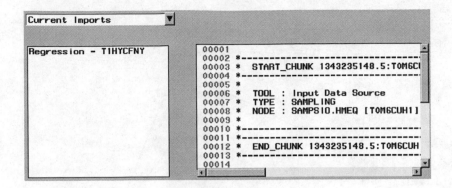

Click the arrow to see the available management functions. By default, the Current Imports are listed. The options include

□ Current imports — (default) lists the scoring code that is currently imported from node predecessors.

□ Accumulated runs — lists the scoring code that is exported by the node's predecessors during the most recent training action. If the training action involves group processing, a separate score entry is listed for each group iteration for each predecessor node. This is the only access to score code that is generated from group processing.

□ Saved — lists saved or merged score code entries.

□ All — lists all score code entries that are managed by the node.

To see the scoring code for a model, double-click a model in the list on the left. The associated scoring code is displayed in the window on the right. The scoring code is a SAS program that performs a SAS DATA step. You can use the scoring code on any system that runs base SAS software. If you modify the settings in a modeling node and run the flow, the scoring code that is associated with the affected model is updated.

To keep modifications in the workspace from affecting the scoring code, you can save the scoring code as follows:

1 From the list on the left, select the name of the model that was used for developing the scoring code. For this example, save the scoring code for the regression model.

2 Right-click the selected model and select **Save**.

3 A dialog box opens that enables you to name the saved source file. You can type a name if you want, although this is not necessary. Type in a name, such as My Regression Code.

4 Press OK. Note the change in the management function from Current Imports to Saved.

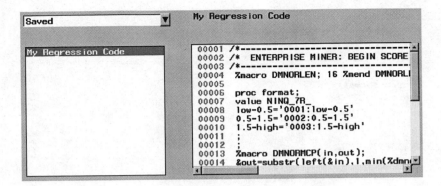

The code is now saved within Enterprise Miner. To use the code outside Enterprise Miner in a SAS session, you need to export the scoring code from Enterprise Miner as follows:

1 Select the name of the code in the list on the left.

2 Right-click the name and select **Export**.

3 Type a name for the saved program such as MYCODE and select Save .

Scoring Using Base SAS

You can use the saved scoring code to score a data set by using base SAS. The program requires only base SAS to run; therefore, you can run the program on any of the systems in which you have installed base SAS whether or not Enterprise Miner is installed.

Enterprise Miner runs on top of a SAS session, and you can use this SAS session at any time. Use this SAS session to score the DMAHMEQ data set in the SAMPSIO library. This is a data set that has all of the inputs for the model. This data set also has response information so that you can compare the predicted outcome to the actual outcome if you want.

To score the data set using SAS, proceed as follows:

1 Select

to make the SAS session active.

2 Select

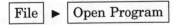

3 Find and select the program that you just saved (named MYCODE in this example). Note: If you used the default folder when you saved the code, the code will be in the same folder that opens when you select

File ► Open Program

4 Select Open . The scoring code appears in the Program Editor of the SAS session. A portion of the code appears below.

```
/*------------------------------------------------------------*/
/*  ENTERPRISE MINER: BEGIN SCORE CODE                        */
/*------------------------------------------------------------*/
%macro DMNORLEN; 16 %mend DMNORLEN;

proc format;
value NINQ_7R_
low-0.5='0001:low-0.5'
0.5-1.5='0002:0.5-1.5'
1.5-high='0003:1.5-high'
;
;
%macro DMNORMCP(in,out);
&out=substr(left(&in),1,min(%dmnorlen,length(left(&in))));
&out=upcase(&out);
%mend DMNORMCP;


%macro DMNORMIP(in);
&in=left(&in);
&in=substr(&in,1,min(%dmnorlen,length(&in)));
&in=upcase(&in);
%mend DMNORMIP;
```

```
DATA &_PREDICT ; SET &_SCORE ;
```

The data set _PREDICT contains the predicted values. The data set that is represented by _SCORE is the data set that you want to score. Since these data sets are being used in a macro (preceded by "&_"), the data sets need to be initialized.

5 Score the DMAHMEQ data set in the SAMPSIO library. To do so, first initialize _PREDICT and _SCORE by placing the following code before the beginning of the scoring code that you opened in step 4:

```
%let _SCORE=SAMPSIO.DMAHMEQ;
%let _PREDICT=X;
```

The second line will initialize _PREDICT. There is actually no X data set. It is just a dummy name. The actual _PREDICT data set is re-created by the scoring code.

6 To see the results of scoring, add the following code at the end of the scoring code that you opened in step 4:

```
PROC PRINT DATA=&_PREDICT;
     VAR BAD P_BAD1 P_BAD0;
run;
```

This code prints the value of BAD as well as P_BAD1 (predicted probability BAD=1) and P_BAD0 (predicted probability BAD=0).

Note: Although it is unnecessary, you might want to sort the observations according to one of the variables, such as P_BAD1. To do so, submit the following code before submitting the PROC PRINT code that was given above. By sorting the observations by descending values of P_BAD1, you arrange the top observations to be those that are most likely to default. △

```
PROC SORT DATA=&_PREDICT;
     BY DESCENDING P_BAD1;
RUN;
```

7 Submit the scoring code by selecting

$\boxed{\text{Run}} \blacktriangleright \boxed{\text{Submit}}$

or by Selecting the Submit icon (🏃) from the toolbox. Inspect the resulting output. The first ten observations of the newly sorted data set are shown below.

Obs	bad	P_BAD1	P_BAD0
1	1	0.99999	.000006728
2	1	0.99992	.000078563
3	1	0.99988	.000117945
4	1	0.99987	.000125720
5	1	0.99985	.000149558
6	1	0.99962	.000384315
7	1	0.99959	.000411150
8	1	0.99946	.000539887
9	1	0.99931	.000687884
10	1	0.99930	.000695732

Observe that since BAD has two levels (0 and 1), P_BAD1+P_BAD0=1. All of the first ten observations represent defaulters, as may have been expected from the high probability of default (shown in P_BAD1).

8 To return to Enterprise Miner, select

$\boxed{\text{Window}} \blacktriangleright \boxed{\text{Score}}$

9 Close the Score node to return to the Diagram Workspace.

Scoring within Enterprise Miner

You have just used the saved scoring code to score a data set by using base SAS. Now score the same data set by using Enterprise Miner. Begin by adding another Input Data Source node to the flow and connect it to the Score node. Add an Insight node and connect the Score node to it as pictured below.

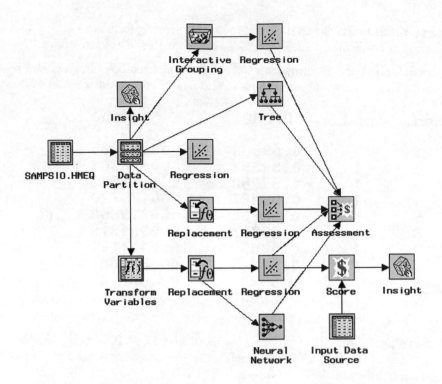

Select the DMAHMEQ data set from SAMPSIO library.

Change the role of the data set from RAW to SCORE.

Role:	RAW ▼	Role:	SCORE ▼

Observe that the data set has 5,960 rows and 13 columns.

Rows:	5,960
Columns:	13

Inspect the variables if you want. There is no need to modify the variables here, since the role and level of each variable is built into the scoring code. After inspection, close this Input Data Source node, and save changes when you are prompted.

Open the Score node. By default, the Score node is inactive when you are running items in a path. Select **Apply training data score code to score data set**. The Score node now adds prediction information to the data set that it is scoring.

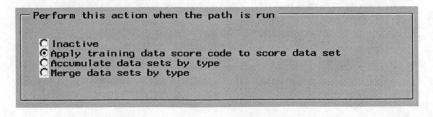

After you request the Score node to apply the scoring data, the Output variables subtab becomes available. This subtab enables you to control what values are added to the scored data set. Select the Output variables subtab and inspect the window that is displayed.

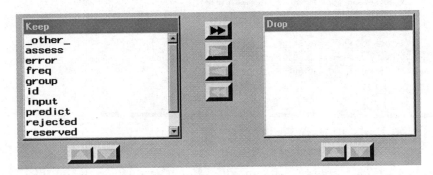

All variables are included by default, but the options that are shown below enable you to drop certain variables if you want. Dropped variables are excluded from the output data set. No variables are dropped in this example.

Close the Score node, saving changes when you are prompted.

Next open the Insight node. Click Select in the Data tab to select the data set to be associated with the score data. This data set typically has an SD prefix that is followed by a string of random alphanumeric characters.

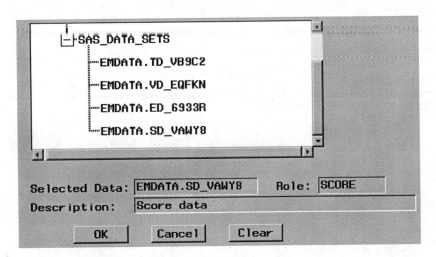

The selected data set is SD_VAWY8 in this example, although the name of your data set will be different. The Description box indicates that this data set represents score data.

Select OK to return to the Data tab of the Insight node. Then close Insight, saving changes when you are prompted. Run Insight and view the results. The scored data set now has 39 variables. Only 13 variables were in the original data set, so the scoring code has added 26 additional variables to this data set. If you want to add only selected variables when scoring, you can specify fewer variables in the Score node as described earlier. The data set that opens has a different name from the one that you selected. Unless you select the option to perform Insight on the entire data set, Insight opens with a sample of 2,000 observations. The prefix SMP_ indicates that it is a sample. You can see some of the newly created variables by scrolling to the right. The scoring code has added missing value indicators as well as prediction information.

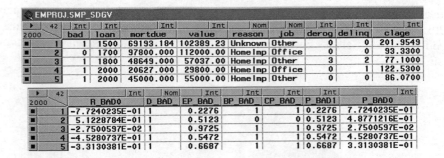

Generating a Report Using the Reporter Node

To create an HTML report, you can add a Reporter node. Add the reporter node after the Assessment node so that the Assessment results are included in the report. Run the flow from the Reporter node. Observe that the nodes become green as the flow is checked, and the nodes become yellow as the report is generated.

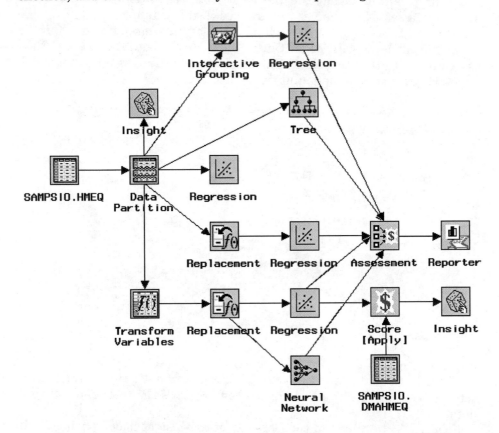

When the run is finished, you can select OK to accept the creation of the HTML report or Open to open the report and view it with your default Internet browser.

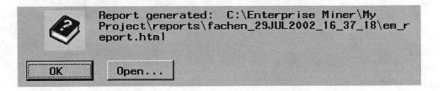

If you do not look at the report, you can view it later by selecting the Reports subtab. The HTML report contains the results from each node in any path that leads to the Reporter node. Some of the results are in the main document, while others are accessible through hyperlinks from the main document. All files that are associated with a report are placed in a folder that is located in the reports folder of the corresponding project folder. The path to the reports folder is shown in the dialog box that is displayed after the report is generated. For example, the dialog box above indicates that the report is located in **C:\Enterprise Miner\My Project\reports\fachen_29JUL2002_16_37_18**, and the main document file is **em_report.html**.

CHAPTER

3

Variable Selection

Introduction to Variable Selection

Data often contains an extremely large number of variables. Using all of the variables in a model is not practical in general, so variable selection plays a critical role in modeling. The previous chapter used stepwise regression to perform variable selection; however, this method may not perform well when you are evaluating data sets that contain hundreds of potential input variables. Furthermore, keep in mind that the stepwise selection method is available only in the Regression node. Variable selection is often more critical for the Neural Network node than it is for other modeling nodes because of the large number of parameters that are generated in relation to using the same number of variables in a regression model.

Because variable selection is a critical phase in model building, Enterprise Miner provides selection methods in two nodes, the Tree node and the Variable Selection node. Variables that are selected by either of these two nodes are immediately available to any subsequent modeling node, including the Regression node.

No single method of selecting variables for use in another modeling tool is uniformly best. It is often useful to consider many types of variable selection in evaluating the importance of each variable.

This chapter demonstrates how to identify important variables by using the Variable Selection node. Although you can also perform variable selection by using the Tree node, that method is not covered here.

For convenience, consider the first flow that you constructed. Add a Variable Selection node after the Replacement node that is connected to the Transform Variables node. Your workspace should now appear as follows:

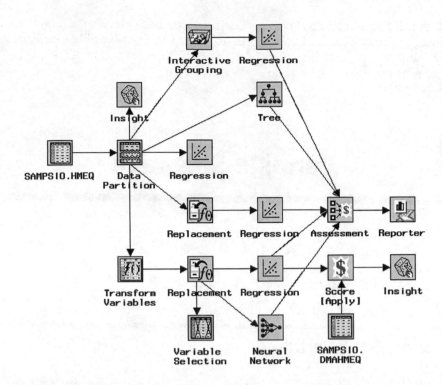

Using the Variable Selection Node

Open the Variable Selection node. The Variables tab is active. A portion of the window is displayed below. Scroll down to see the missing value indicator variables.

Name	Status	Model Role	Measurement
BAD	use	target	binary
LOAN	use	input	interval
MORTDUE	use	input	interval
VALUE	use	input	interval
REASON	use	input	binary
JOB	use	input	nominal
DEROG	use	input	interval
DELINQ	use	input	interval
CLAGE	use	input	interval
CLNO	use	input	interval
DEBTINC	use	input	interval
INDELINQ	use	input	interval
INDEROG	use	input	interval
YOJ_IYNC	use	input	interval
NINQ_7RJ	use	input	ordinal
M_LOAN	don't use	rejected	unary
M_MORTDU	don't use	rejected	binary

Observe that the missing value indicators have **rejected** listed for Model Role; these indicators are rejected by default, and therefore their Status is set to **don't use**. If you want to identify which (if any) of the missing value indicators would be useful in prediction, you must change their Status to **use**. The missing value indicators that have a unary measurement level will not be useful since unary indicates that every observation in the data set has the same value.

Change the Status of all of the missing indicator variables to **use**. Variables that have the unary measurement level are dropped automatically.

Note: You will not see the missing value indicator variables unless you have previously run the Replacement node. △

Select the Manual Selection tab. A portion of the window is displayed below.

Name	Measurement	Role Assignment
DEBTINC	interval	<automatic>
INDELINQ	interval	<automatic>
INDEROG	interval	<automatic>
YOJ_IYNC	interval	<automatic>
NINQ_7RJ	ordinal	<automatic>
M_LOAN	unary	<automatic>

This tab enables you to force variables to be included or excluded from future analyses. By default, the role assignment is **automatic**, which means that the role is set based on the analysis that is performed in this node. All variables whose status was set to **use** appear in this tab. If you want to ensure that a variable is included, specify the Role Assignment as **input**.

Selecting Variables Using the R-square Criterion

Select the Target Associations tab. This tab enables you to choose one of two selection criteria and specify options for the chosen criterion. By default, the node removes variables that are unrelated to the target (according to the settings that are used for the selection criterion) and scores the data sets. Consider the settings that are associated with the default R-square criterion first.

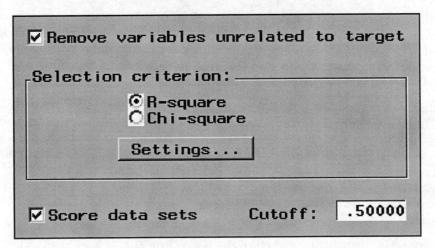

Because R-square is already selected as the selection criterion, click Settings on the Target Associations tab.

```
Squared correlation      <  .00500

Stepwise R2 improvement  <  .00050

☐ Include 2-way interactions

☐ Bin interval variables (AOV16)

☑ Use only grouped class variables

                          OK      Cancel
```

The R-square criterion uses a goodness-of-fit criterion to evaluate variables. It uses a stepwise method of selecting variables that stops when the improvement in the R^2 value is less than 0.00050. By default, the method rejects variables whose contribution is less than 0.005.

The following three-step process is done when you apply the R-square variable selection criterion to a binary target. If the target is nonbinary, only the first two steps are performed.

1 Enterprise Miner computes the squared correlation (R^2) for each variable with the target and then assigns the rejected role to those variables that have a value less than the Squared correlation criterion (default 0.00500).

2 Enterprise Miner evaluates the remaining significant (chosen) variables by using a forward stepwise R^2 regression. Variables that have a stepwise R^2 improvement less than the threshold criterion (default 0.00050) are assigned to the rejected role.

3 For binary targets, Enterprise Miner performs a logistic regression by using the predicted values that are output from the forward stepwise regression as the independent input variable.

Additional options on the Settings tab enable you to

☐ **Include 2-way interactions** — when selected, this option requests Enterprise Miner to create and evaluate 2-way interactions for categorical inputs.

☐ **Bin interval variables** — when selected, this option requests Enterprise Miner to bin interval variables into 16 equally spaced groups (AOV16) . The AOV16 variables are created to help identify nonlinear relationships with the target. Bins that contain zero observations are eliminated. This means that an AOV16 variable can have fewer than 16 bins.

☐ **Use only grouped class variables** — when this option is selected, Enterprise Miner uses only the grouped class variable to evaluate variable importance. A grouped class variable might or might not have fewer levels than the original class variables. To create the grouped variable, Enterprise Miner attempts to combine levels of the variable with similar behavior. Deselecting this option requests Enterprise Miner to use the grouped class variable as well as the original class variable in evaluating variable importance, which may greatly increase processing time.

Use the default settings and close the node. Run the flow from the Variable Selection node and view the results. The Variables tab is active. To see the results more easily, click the **Name** column heading. Then click the **Role** column heading to sort by role. Inspect the results.

Name	Role	Rejection Reason
CLAGE	input	
DEBTINC	input	
DELINQ	input	
DEROG	input	
G_JOB	input	
INDELINQ	input	
INDEROG	input	
NINQ_7RJ	input	
YOJ_IYNC	input	
CLNO	rejected	Low R2 w/ target
JOB	rejected	Group variable G_JOB preferred
LOAN	rejected	Low R2 w/ target
MORTDUE	rejected	Low R2 w/ target

Observe that CLAGE, DEBTINC, DELINQ, DEROG, G_JOB, INDELINQ, INDEROG, NINQ_7RJ, and YOJ_IYNC are retained. Note that G_JOB is the grouped version of the JOB variable, and INDELINQ, INDEROG, NINQ_7RJ, and YOJ_IYNC are the transformed DELINQ, DEROG, NINQ, and YOJ variables, respectively. The role of the missing value indicators is set to **rejected** because this was the default for missing value indicator variables in the Replacement node. If you want to use these missing value indicators in subsequent nodes, change the role of these variables to **input** in the node that you want to run.

To see the impact of performing variable selection, connect the Variable Selection node to the Neural Network node. Follow these steps.

1 Delete the connection between the Replacement node and the Neural Network node by selecting the line segment and pressing the Backspace or Delete key. Optionally, right-click the line and select **Delete** from the pop-up menu.

2 Add a connection between the Variable Selection node and the Neural Network node.

Inspect the resulting process flow

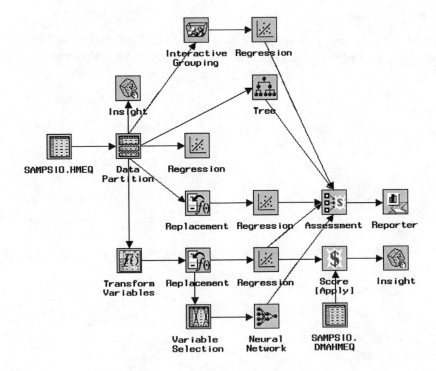

It is highly recommended that you perform some type of variable selection before proceeding in building Neural Network models. Neural Network models are very flexible, but they are also very computationally intensive. Failure to reduce the number of input variables may result in

□ an overfit model that does not perform well in practice

□ a tremendous increase in the computational time that is necessary to fit a model

□ computational difficulties in obtaining good parameter estimates.

Open the Neural Network node. The Variables tab is active.

Name	Status	Model Role	Measurement	Type	Format
G_JOB	use	input	nominal	num	best12.
INDELINQ	use	input	interval	num	BEST12.
INDEROG	use	input	interval	num	BEST12.
JOB	don't use	rejected	nominal	char	$7.
LOAN	don't use	rejected	interval	num	BEST12.
MORTDUE	don't use	rejected	interval	num	BEST12.
M_CLAGE	don't use	rejected	binary	num	BEST12.
M_CLNO	don't use	rejected	binary	num	BEST12.
M_DEBTIN	don't use	rejected	binary	num	BEST12.
M_DELINQ	don't use	rejected	binary	num	BEST12.
M_DEROG	don't use	rejected	binary	num	BEST12.

Observe that many of the variables have their status set to **don't use**. Change the status for M_VALUE, M_DEROG, and M_DELINQ to **use** before proceeding. In previous investigations, these three missing value indicator variables were selected for inclusion in the final model. You could use the variable JOB instead of the grouped variable G_JOB by setting the status for JOB to **use** and the status for G_JOB to **don't use**, but that is not done here. Close the Neural Network node, and save changes when you are prompted. Then run the flow from the Assessment node and view the results when you are prompted.

Build a lift chart that compares all of the models by highlighting all of the rows to select them and then selecting

| Tools | ▶ | Lift Chart. |

The neural network shows some improvement in the first decile, although the stepwise regression model and decision tree still outperform the neural network.

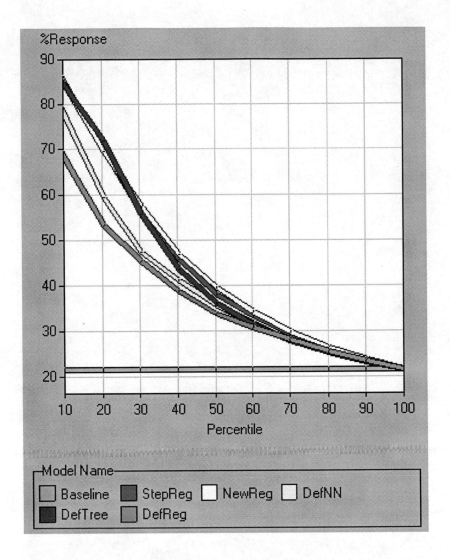

The output above is labeled by model names. To see the model names, select the following items from the lift chart window.

Format ▶ Model Name

You may need to maximize the window or resize the legend to see all of the model names.

As an exercise, consider revisiting the Variable Selection node and using the Chi-square criteria instead of the R-square criteria.

CHAPTER

4

Clustering Tools

Problem Formulation

Consider the following scenario. A baseball manager wants to identify and group players on the team who are very similar with respect to several statistics of interest. Note that there is no response variable in this example. The manager simply wants to identify different groups of players. The manager also wants to learn what differentiates players in one group from players in a different group.

The data is located in the DMABASE data set in the SAMPSIO library. The following table contains description of key variables.

Table 4.1   Descriptions of Selected Variables in the DMABASE Data Set

Name	Model Role	Measurement Level	Description
NAME	ID	Nominal	Player Name
TEAM	Rejected	Nominal	Team at the end of 1986
POSITION	Rejected	Nominal	Positions played in 1986
LEAGUE	Rejected	Binary	League at the end of 1986
DIVISION	Rejected	Binary	Division at the end of 1986
NO_ATBAT	Input	Interval	Times at Bat in 1986
NO_HITS	Input	Interval	Hits in 1986

Name	Model Role	Measurement Level	Description
NO_HOME	Input	Interval	Home Runs in 1986
NO_RUNS	Input	Interval	Runs in 1986
NO_RBI	Input	Interval	RBIs in 1986
NO_BB	Input	Interval	Walks in 1986
YR_MAJOR	Input	Interval	Years in the Major Leagues
CR_ATBAT	Input	Interval	Career Times at Bat
CR_HITS	Input	Interval	Career Hits
CR_HOME	Input	Interval	Career Home Runs
CR_RUNS	Input	Interval	Career Runs
CR_RBI	Input	Interval	Career RBIs
CR_BB	Input	Interval	Career Walks
NO_OUTS	Input	Interval	Put Outs in 1986
NO_ASSTS	Input	Interval	Assists in 1986
NO_ERROR	Input	Interval	Errors in 1986
SALARY	Rejected	Interval	1987 Salary in Thousands
LOGSALAR	Input	Interval	Log of 1987 Salary in Thousands

For this example, you will set the model role for TEAM, POSITION, LEAGUE, DIVISION, and SALARY to **rejected**. Set the model role for SALARY to **rejected** since this information is stored in LOGSALAR in the data set. No target variables are used in generating a cluster analysis or self-organizing Map (SOM). If you want to identify groups based on a target variable, consider a predictive modeling technique and specify a categorical target.

Overview of Clustering Methods

Cluster analysis is often referred to as supervised classification because it attempts to predict group or class membership for a specific categorical response variable. *Clustering*, on the other hand, is referred to as unsupervised classification because it identifies groups or classes within the data based on all the input variables. These groups, or clusters, are assigned numbers; however, the cluster number cannot be used to evaluate the proximity between clusters. Self-organizing maps (SOMs) attempt to create clusters and plot the resulting clusters on a map so that cluster proximity can be evaluated graphically, but that is not considered here.

Building the Initial Flow

Assemble the following diagram and connect the nodes as shown.

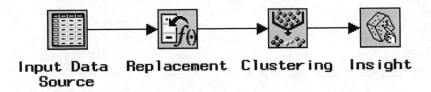

Input Data   Replacement Clustering Insight
Source

Setting Up the Input Data Source Node

1 Open the Input Data Source node.
2 Select the DMABASE data set from the SAMPSIO library.
3 Set the model role for NAME to **id**, and set the model role for TEAM, POSITION, LEAGUE, DIVISION, and SALARY to **rejected**.
4 Explore the distributions and descriptive statistics as you want.
5 Select the Interval Variables tab and observe that the only variables that have missing values are SALARY and LOGSALAR. Select the Class Variables tab and observe that there are no missing values. None of the class variables have been included in this example. As an exercise, consider retracing the upcoming steps after using LEAGUE as an input variable.
6 Close the Input Data Source node, saving changes when you are prompted.

When to Use the Replacement Node

Although it is not always necessary to impute missing values, at times the amount of missing data may prevent the Clustering node from obtaining a cluster solution. The Clustering node needs some complete observations in order to generate the initial clusters. When the amount of missing data is too extreme, use the Replacement node to impute the missing values. Although it was not necessary, this strategy was used for demonstration in this example.

Setting Up the Clustering Node

1 Open the Clustering node. The Variables tab is active. K-means clustering is very sensitive to the scale of measurement of different inputs. Consequently, it is recommended that you use one of the standardization options if the data has not been standardized previously in the flow.
2 Select **StdDev.** on the Variables tab.

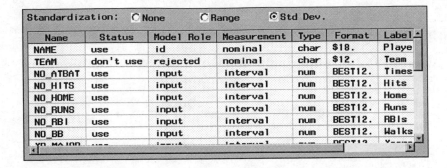

3 Select the Clusters tab.

4 Observe that the default method for choosing the number of clusters is **Automatic**.

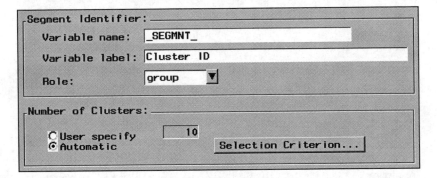

By default, the Clustering node uses the Cubic Clustering Criterion (CCC) that is based on a sample of 2,000 observations to estimate the appropriate number of clusters. You can change the default sample size by selecting the Data tab and then selecting the Preliminary Training and Profiles tab. This example has only 322 observations, so all of the observations are used. The clustering algorithm determines a ten-cluster solution (by default). You can specify a different number of initial clusters by selecting Selection Criterion, but that is not done here. The algorithm then clusters the remaining clusters until all of the observations are in one cluster.

5 Close the Clustering node, saving changes when you are prompted.

Interpreting the Results

Run the diagram from the Clustering node and view the results. The Partition tab in the Results window is active.

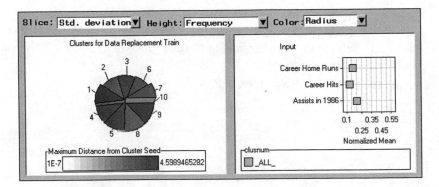

It is easy to see that the Clustering node chose a ten-cluster solution. The baseball manager feels that this many clusters may be hard to interpret, and decides to limit the search to between two and ten clusters. The algorithm now generates a ten-cluster solution initially, and then it clusters the groups from the initial solution until all of the observations are in one cluster. These clusters are typically slightly different from those obtained earlier.

Close the Clustering node results window.

Limiting the Number of Clusters

To limit the number of clusters,

1 Open the Clustering node.

2 Select the Clusters tab.

3 Select **Selection Criterion** in the Number of Clusters section.

4 Type **10** for the Maximum Number of Clusters.

5 Click [OK].

6 Close the Clustering node, saving changes when you are prompted.

Rerun the flow from the Clustering node and view the results. The Clustering node returns a three-cluster solution.

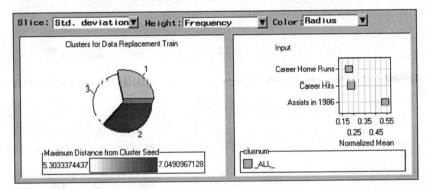

Examining the Three Clusters

The manager decides to investigate this solution further. Select the Tilt icon (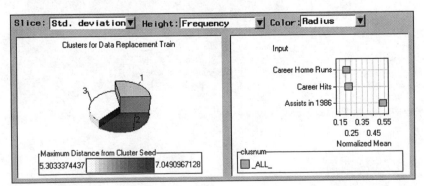) from the toolbar and tilt the three-dimensional pie chart as shown below.

Inspect the chart in the left window of the Partition tab.

Clusters for Data Replacement Train

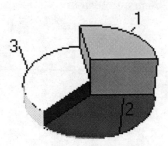

┌─Maximum Distance from Cluster Seed──────────────┐
│ 5.3033374437 [gradient bar] 7.0490967128 │
└───┘

This chart summarizes three statistics of the three clusters. The options at the top of the Partition tab indicate that the

- ☐ size of the slice is proportional to the cluster standard deviation
- ☐ height of the slice is related to the number of observations in the cluster
- ☐ color indicates the radius (distance from the cluster center to the most remote observation in that cluster).

You can make some general observations that are based on this plot, including

- ☐ Cluster 1 contains the most cases, followed by cluster 3 and cluster 2.
- ☐ Cluster 3 has the smallest radius, while cluster 2 has the largest radius.

You can use the Tilt and Rotate tools to position the chart to evaluate wedge size, but that is not done here. Next, consider the right side of the window. It is often useful to maximize the window to see as much of the graph as possible.

Inspect the right side of the window. You may need to use the Move Graph tool

( ) to see all of the variable labels.

Input

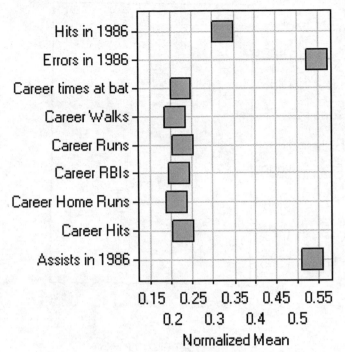

The right side of the window shows the normalized means for each input variable (mean divided by its standard deviation). Observe that not all of the variable labels are visible. Depending on your screen and window settings, you may see only some (or none) of these variables.

To see the other variables, select the Scroll Data tool ( ) from the toolbar and drag the pointer in the plot. For example, scrolling to the top of the chart yields the following normalized mean. Inspect the plot.

Input

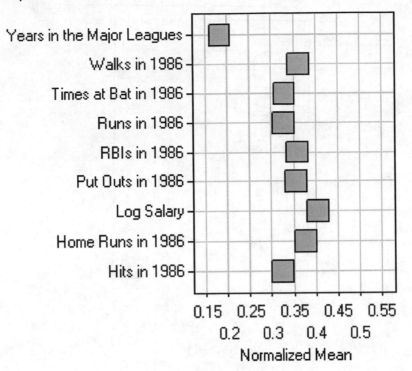

The normalized mean plot can be used to compare the overall normalized means with the normalized means in each cluster. To do so,

1 Select the Select Points icon (⬚) from the toolbar.

2 Select one of the clusters by clicking the desired wedge in the three-dimensional pie chart. The example below shows the results for cluster 1.

3 Select the Refresh Input Means Plot icon (⬚) from the toolbar.

After scrolling to the top of the plot, inspect the Normalized Mean Plot.

Input

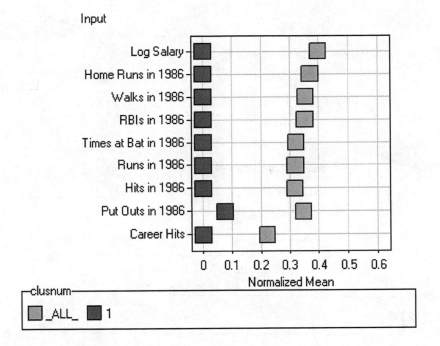

The dark squares indicate the normalized means for the selected cluster and the light squares represent the overall normalized means. Note that cluster 1 has values that are far below the average with respect to all of the variables that are shown above. If you scroll through the plot by using the Scroll Data tool, you will find that the players in cluster 1 are below the mean for all of the variables.

Consider the players in cluster 2. To do so,

1 Select the Select Points icon ( ) from the toolbar.

2 Select cluster 2 in the three-dimensional pie chart.

3 Select the Refresh Input Means Plot icon ( ) from the toolbar.

4 Use the Scroll Data tool and scroll to the top of the output and inspect the resulting plot.

Inspect the plot for cluster 2.

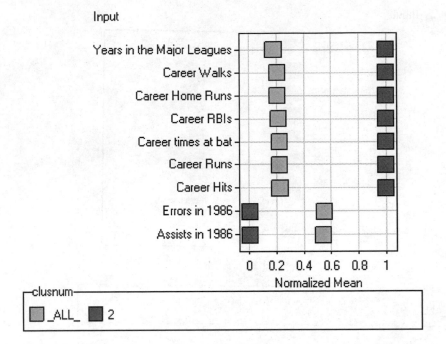

Cluster 2 contains players who have higher than average career statistics and lower than average errors and assists in 1986. Scroll down to see the remaining variables.

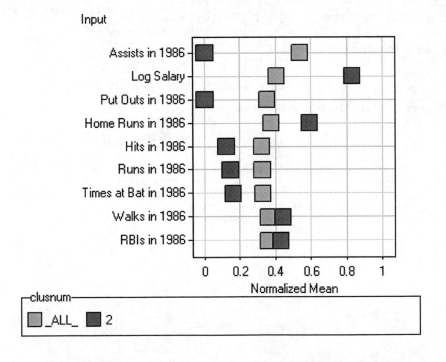

Cluster 2 players are also lower than average for their 1986 put outs, hits, runs, and times at bat. These players are higher on 1986 salary, home runs, walks, and RBIs.
Inspect the players in cluster 3 in a similar fashion.
Investigate the report for the cluster 3 players.

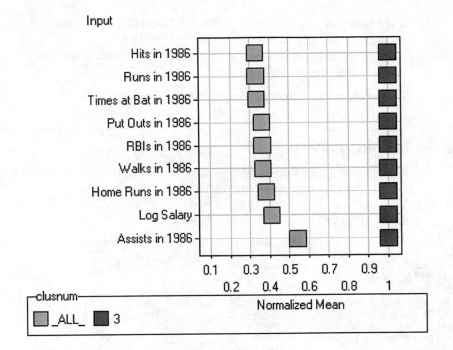

Cluster 3 players are much higher than average on their yearly statistics and salary.

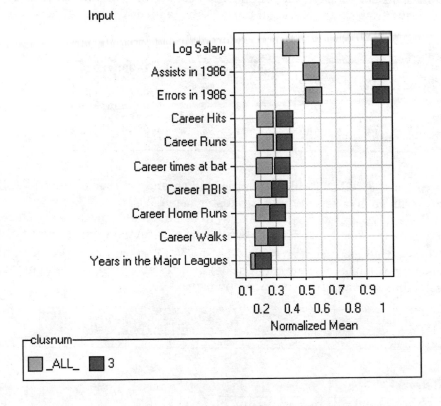

The career statistics for cluster 3 players are somewhat higher than average, and they have been in the major leagues an average number of years.

An admittedly oversimplified description for these clusters would suggest that

☐ Cluster 1 players are young players who have relatively little experience and relatively low lifetime and 1986 statistics.

□ Cluster 2 players are older players who have relatively high lifetime statistics but somewhat average (or below average) 1986 statistics.

□ Cluster 3 players have a fair amount of experience and have somewhat average lifetime statistics but high 1986 statistics.

Close the Clustering node when you have finished exploring the results.

Using the Insight Node

The Insight node can also be used to compare the differences among the attributes of the prospects. Open the Insight node and select **Entire data set** from the Data tab's Insight Based On section. Close the Insight node, saving changes when you are prompted. Run the flow from the Insight node and view the results.

	name	team	no_atbat	no_hits
	Nom	Nom	Int	Int
1	Allanson, Andy	Cleveland	293	66
2	Ashby, Alan	Houston	315	81
3	Davis, Alan	Seattle	479	130
4	Dawson, Andre	Montreal	496	141
5	Galarraga, Andres	Montreal	321	87
6	Griffin, Alfredo	Oakland	594	169
7	Newman, Al	Montreal	185	37

All of the observations in the original data set are present, but the number of columns has increased from 23 to 25. Scroll to the right to identify the two new columns.

	no_error	salary	logsalar	_SEGMNT_	distance
	Int	Int	Int	Int	Int
1	20	.	5.9272	1	3.1433942072
2	10	475.000	6.1633	1	2.7064870361
3	14	480.000	6.1738	3	3.0773462954
4	3	500.000	6.2146	3	3.0806907246
5	4	91.500	4.5163	1	3.0854258867
6	25	750.000	6.6201	3	4.3658691857
7	7	70.000	4.2485	1	3.3412165642

The column _SEGMNT_ identifies the cluster, and another column identifies the distance from each observation to its cluster mean.

Use the analytical tools within Insight to evaluate and compare the clusters. Begin by looking at the yearly statistics. Here is one way to make these comparisons:

1 Change the measurement scale for _SEGMNT_ from interval to nominal by clicking **Int** (the measurement scale) directly above the variable name, and then selecting **Nominal** from the pop-up menu.

	no_error	salary	logsalar	_SEGMNT_	distance
	Int	Int	Int	Nom	Int
1	20	.	5.9272	1	3.1433942072

2 Select

| Analyze | ▶ | Box Plot/Mosaic Plot |

3 Highlight the variables NO_ATBATS through NO_BB to select them. You can do this by dragging through the list or by selecting NO_ATBATS and then SHIFT-clicking on NO_BB.

4 Click Ⓨ.

5 Scroll to the bottom and select _SEGMENT_.

6 Click $\boxed{\text{X}}$.

7 Select $\boxed{\text{OK}}$.

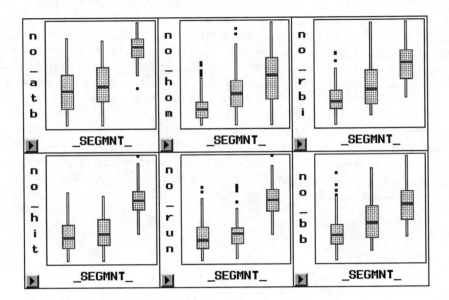

Cluster 3 is high on all of these statistics. Clusters 1 and 2 perform more similarly with respect to these statistics.

Investigate the career statistics as well by evaluating YR_MAJOR through CR_BB.

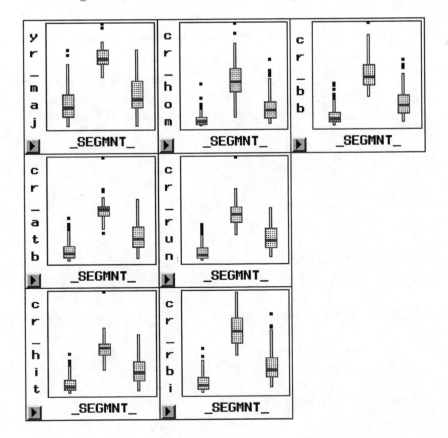

Observe that cluster 2 is high on most of these career statistics while clusters 1 and 3 are similar to each other.

Note that this type of plot works only for variables that have the same measurement level. The plots above are displayed for variables that are identified as interval variables (**Int**) in the Insight data table. If you try to specify both nominal and interval variables as Y when you select a **Box Plot/Mosaic Plot**, Insight returns an error. You must look at the nominal variables together and the interval variables together. You can have multiple plots open at the same time, however, so this does not pose a problem.

In addition, note that only a subset of the variables was used at one time. Insight sizes the plots based on the number of plots. Selecting too many variables results in the generation of many small plots, which may be difficult to read. While resizing individual graphs is easy, resizing all of them is more time-consuming, so it is best to look at specific subsets when you are plotting.

Generating several cluster solutions is fairly easy, but interpreting a particular cluster solution can be extremely challenging. In some cases no easy or useful cluster interpretation is possible. Since clusters naturally partition the population into mutually exclusive sets, they may provide some benefit even if a convenient interpretation is not readily available.

CHAPTER

5

Association Analysis

Problem Formulation

Consider the following scenario. A store wants to examine its customer base and to understand which of its products tend to be purchased together. It has chosen to conduct a market-basket analysis of a sample of its customer base.

The ASSOCS data set lists the grocery products that are purchased by 1,001 customers. Twenty possible items are represented:

Table 5.1   Selected Variables in the ASSOCS Data Set

Code	Product
apples	apples
artichok	artichokes
avocado	avocado
baguette	baguettes
bordeaux	wine
bourbon	bourbon
chicken	chicken
coke	cola
corned_b	corned beef
cracker	cracker
ham	ham
heineken	beer
herring	fish
ice_crea	ice cream
olives	olives
peppers	peppers

Code	Product
sardines	sardines
soda	soda water
steak	steak
turkey	turkey

Seven items were purchased by each of 1,001 customers, which yields 7,007 rows in the data set. Each row of the data set represents a customer-product combination. In most data sets, not all customers have the same number of products.

Building the Initial Flow

Construct the following diagram.

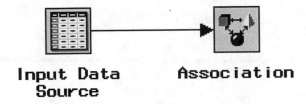

Input Data   **Association**
Source

Setting Up the Input Data Source Node

1 Open the Input Data Source node.
2 Select the ASSOCS data set from the SAMPSIO library.
3 Click the Variables tab.
4 Set the model role for CUSTOMER to `id`.
5 Set the model role for PRODUCT to `target`.
6 Set the model role for TIME to `rejected`.

   Note: TIME is a variable that identifies the sequence in which the products were purchased. In this example, all of the products were purchased at the same time, so the order relates only to the order in which they are priced at the register. When order is taken into account, association analysis is known as *sequence analysis*. Sequence analysis is not demonstrated here. △

7 Close and save changes to the Input Data Source node.

Setting Up the Association Node

Open the Association node. The Variables tab is active by default. Inspect the tab.

Name	Status	Model Role	Measurement	Type	Informat
CUSTOMER	use	id	interval	num	12.
PRODUCT	use	target	nominal	char	$8.

Select the General tab. This tab enables you to modify the analysis mode and control how many rules are generated.

```
Analysis mode:        ⦿ By Context    ○ Association   ○ Sequences

┌─Minimum Transaction Frequency to Support Associations:────────────┐
│  ⦿ 5% of largest single item frequency                            │
│  ○ Specify as a percentage:                        ┌──────────┐ % │
│  ○ Specify a count:                                └──────────┘   │
└───────────────────────────────────────────────────────────────────┘


   Maximum number of items in an association:    ┌──────┐
                                                 │   4  │
                                                 └──────┘

   Minimum confidence for rule generation:    ┌────┐
                                              │ 10 │ %
                                              └────┘
```

Understanding and Choosing Analysis Modes

Inspect the Analysis mode portion of this dialog box.

```
Analysis mode:        ⦿ By Context    ○ Association   ○ Sequences
```

The default analysis mode is **By Context**. This mode uses information that is specified in the Input Data Source node to determine the appropriate analysis. If the input data set contains

- □ an ID variable and a target variable, the node automatically performs an association analysis.

- □ a sequence variable that has a status of use, the node performs a sequence analysis. A sequence analysis requires the specification of a variable whose model role is **sequence**. An association analysis ignores this ordering.

Other options that are available in the General tab include

- □ Minimum Transaction Frequency to Support Associations - specifies a minimum level of support to claim that items are associated (that is, they occur together in the database). The default frequency is 5%.

- □ Maximum number of items in an association - determines the maximum size of the item set to be considered. For example, the default of four items indicates that up to four-way associations are performed.

- □ Minimum confidence for rule generation - specifies the minimum confidence to generate a rule. The default level is 10%. This option is unavailable if you are performing a sequence analysis.

For this example, use the default Association settings. Close the Association node. Since you did not make any changes, you should not be prompted to save the changes. If you are prompted to save changes, select No. Run the diagram from the Association node and view the results.

The Rules tab is displayed first.

	Relations	Lift	Support(%)	Confidence(%)	Transaction Count	Rule
1	2	1.25	36.56	61.00	366.00	heineken ==> cracker
2	2	1.25	36.56	75.00	366.00	cracker ==> heineken
3	2	1.11	26.07	43.50	261.00	heineken ==> baguette
4	2	1.11	26.07	66.58	261.00	baguette ==> heineken
5	2	1.35	25.67	80.82	257.00	soda ==> heineken
6	2	1.35	25.67	42.83	257.00	heineken ==> soda
7	2	1.11	25.57	54.12	256.00	olives ==> hering
8	2	1.11	25.57	52.67	256.00	hering ==> olives
9	2	1.38	25.17	42.00	252.00	heineken ==> artichok
10	2	1.38	25.17	82.62	252.00	artichok ==> heineken

The Rules tab contains information for each rule. Consider the rule A => B in which A and B each represent one product, and then observe the following:

- Support (%) for A => B is the percentage of all customers who purchased both A and B. Support is a measure of how frequently the rule occurs in the database.

- Confidence (%) for A => B is the percentage of all customers who purchased both A and B, divided by the number of customers who purchased A.

- Lift of A => B is a measure of strength of the association. If Lift=2 for the rule A => B, then a customer having A is twice as likely to have B as a customer chosen at random.

Right-click the **Support(%)** column and select

Sort ► Descending.

	Relations	Lift	Support(%)	Confidence(%)	Transaction Count	Rule
1	2	1.25	36.56	61.00	366.00	heineken ==> cracker
2	2	1.25	36.56	75.00	366.00	cracker ==> heineken
3	2	1.11	26.07	66.58	261.00	baguette ==> heineken
4	2	1.11	26.07	43.50	261.00	heineken ==> baguette
5	2	1.35	25.67	80.82	257.00	soda ==> heineken
6	2	1.35	25.67	42.83	257.00	heineken ==> soda
7	2	1.11	25.57	52.67	256.00	hering ==> olives
8	2	1.11	25.57	54.12	256.00	olives ==> hering
9	2	1.38	25.17	82.62	252.00	artichok ==> heineken
10	2	1.38	25.17	42.00	252.00	heineken ==> artichok

Recall that Support(%) is the percentage of customers who have all the services that are involved in the rule. For example, 36.56% of the 1,001 customers purchased crackers and beer (rule 1), 25.57% purchased olives and herring (rule 7).

Consider the Confidence(%) column above.

Confidence(%) represents the percentage of customers who have the right-hand side (RHS) item among those who have the left-hand side (LHS) item. For example, of the customers who purchased crackers, 75% purchased beer (rule 2). Of the customers who purchased beer, however, only 61% purchased crackers (rule 1).

Lift, in the context of association rules, is the ratio of the confidence of a rule to the confidence of a rule, assuming that the RHS was independent of the LHS. Consequently, lift is a measure of association between the LHS and RHS of the rule. Values that are greater than one represent positive association between the LHS and RHS. Values that are equal to one represent independence. Values that are less than one represent a negative association between the LHS and RHS.

Click the **Lift** column with the right mouse button and select

Sort ► Descending.

	Relations	Lift	Support(%)	Confidence(%)	Transaction Count	Rule
1	4	5.67	8.99	71.43	90.00	peppers & avocado ==> sardines & apples
2	4	5.67	8.99	71.43	90.00	sardines & apples ==> peppers & avocado
3	4	5.64	11.59	82.86	116.00	ice_crea & chicken ==> sardines & coke
4	4	5.64	11.59	78.91	116.00	sardines & coke ==> ice_crea & chicken
5	4	5.57	9.59	66.21	96.00	ice_crea & bourbon ==> turkey & coke
6	4	5.57	9.59	80.67	96.00	turkey & coke ==> ice_crea & bourbon
7	4	5.53	11.59	83.45	116.00	coke & chicken ==> sardines & ice_crea
8	4	5.53	11.59	76.82	116.00	sardines & ice_crea ==> coke & chicken
9	4	5.48	9.09	72.22	91.00	peppers & avocado ==> sardines & baguette
10	4	5.48	9.09	68.94	91.00	sardines & baguette ==> peppers & avocado

The lift for rule 1 indicates that a customer who buys peppers and avocados is about 5.67 times as likely to purchase sardines and apples as a customer taken at random. The Support(%) for this rule, unfortunately, is very low (8.99%), indicating that the event in which all four products are purchased together is a relatively rare occurrence.

CHAPTER

6

Link Analysis

Problem Formulation

Consider the following scenario. As part of your business, you sell books and other publications from your Web site. Your Web log data contains information about the navigation patterns that visitors make within your Web site. You want to examine the files that are requested. In addition, you want to determine the most commonly occurring paths that visitors take from your home page to the checkout page. In other words, you want to what paths visitors are taking when they make a purchase.

The data is located in the DMWEB data set in the SAMPSIO library. The following table contains descriptions of the variables.

Table 6.1   Description of Variables in the DMWEB Data Set

Name	Model Role	Measurement Level	Description
REFERRER	Rejected	Nominal	Referring URL
REQUESTED_FILE	Target	Nominal	File that the visitor clicked
SESSION_IDENTIFIER	ID	Nominal	Unique ID code for the session
SESSION_SEQUENCE	Sequence	Interval	Order in which files were requested within a session

Examining Web Log Data

The following example enables you to examine the Web log data.

Setting Up the Diagram

Construct the following diagram:

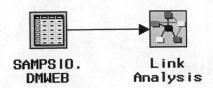

SAMPSIO.
DMWEB

Link
Analysis

Specify the settings for the Input Data Source node:

1 Open the Input Data Source node.

2 Select the DMWEB data set from the SAMPSIO library.

3 Click the Variables tab.

4 Set the Model Role for REFERRER to **rejected**.

5 Set the Model Role for REQUESTED_FILE to**target**.

6 Set the Model Role for SESSION_IDENTIFIER to **id**.

7 Set the Model Role for SESSION_SEQUENCE to **sequence**.

8 Close and save the changes to the Input Data Source node.

Open the Link Analysis node. The Variables tab is open by default. Click the

Settings icon (   ) from the toolbar.
The Detailed Settings window opens.

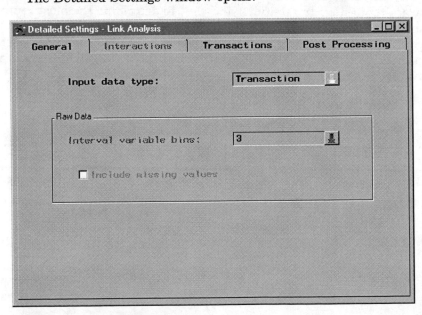

The General tab is active by default. The **Input data type** is set as **Transaction** because the input data set contains a target variable and an ID variable.

Select the Transactions tab.

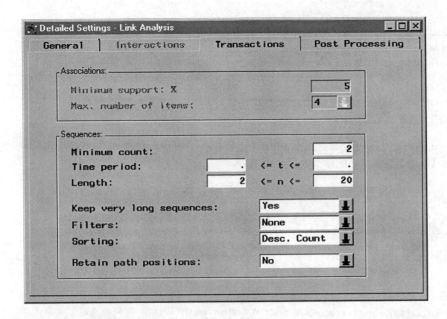

This tab enables you to determine what kinds of sequences are used in the analysis. Specify the settings in the Transactions tab:

1 Set the **Minimum Count** to **1**.

2 Set **Retain path positions** to **Yes**.

You set the **Minimum Count** to **1** because you want to ensure that you analyze all visits to your Web site, including those visitors who requested only a single page. You set **Retain path positions** to **Yes** because you want to keep the structure of your data intact when you determine the paths that visitors take when they navigate your Web site.

Click the Post Processing tab.

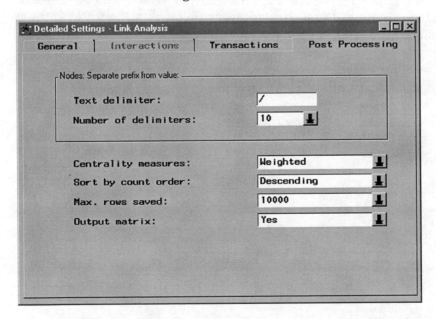

Set the **Number of delimiters** to the maximum value of **10**. This option separates the URL string into the directory path and value strings. Use the maximum value because some of the URLs contain up to ten path and value strings.

Close the Detailed Settings window, and close the Link Analysis node, saving your changes when you are prompted.

Run the diagram from the Link Analysis Node and view the results.

Viewing the Results

After you run the Link Analysis node, click ⌈Yes⌉ when you are prompted to view the results. The Output tab is displayed first.

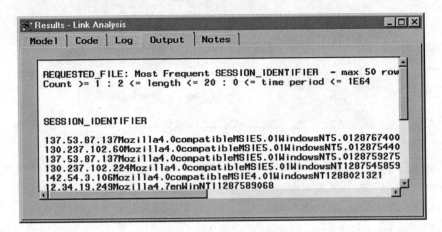

The Output tab displays the SAS output of the Link Analysis run. You can view the results of the sequence analysis that the node performed, as well as information about the NODES and LINKS data sets that the node creates.

Click the Detailed Results icon (   ) to open the Link Analysis Viewer window. By default, the Link Graph tab of the Link Analysis Viewer window is active. The nodes and links are arranged in a circular layout. Right-click the workspace (not a node or link) and select **Info** from the pop-up menu. The Link Analysis Information window opens.

```
Link Analysis Information                              _ □ ×
.
Nodes:
      Data Set:          EMPROJ.NOD_X9XY
      Rows Total:        388
      Rows Retrieved:    32
      Variables:         c1 c2 value var count id text prefix
         Color:          var
         Size:           count
         Shape:          role
         Layout:         var
         Cluster:
.
Links:
      Data Set:          EMPROJ.LIN_UOFI
      Rows Total:        664
      Rows Retrieved:    46
      Variables:         count percent count1 id1 count2 id2 li
         Value:          count
         Direction:      dir
.
      View Batchsize:    256
      Batch Start:       1
      Batch Stop:        46
      Number Hidden:     0
      Mask Attribute:    LAYOUT_MASK
      Display Mode:      MASK
```

Examine the window. The Link Analysis Information window displays information about the nodes and links. In the Nodes section of the window, note that 32 rows were retrieved. This indicates that the current display is showing only 32 nodes. However, the entire NODES data set contains 388 rows. Because you are using Web log data, you want to include as many nodes as possible so that all of the URLs in your data set are used. In addition, the default circular layout is not the best technique to use if you want to view Web log data. The following section describes how you can better visualize your data.

Showing Paths

To create a polar tree view of the results

1 Right-click the workspace within the **Link Graph** tab and select

   Remove ► All

   from the pop-up menu.

2 Right-click the workspace and select

   Add ► All

   from the pop-up menu.

3 In the Layout window, select **Tree** from the **Technique** drop-down list. Use the default values in the **Node Grouping** and **Link Value** boxes. Click OK.

4 In the Tree Options window, select **Polar** from the **Orientation** drop-down list and click OK.

View the new polar tree layout.

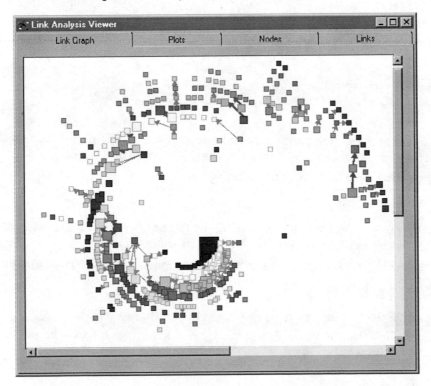

The size of each node in the layout is determined by the count of the node. Because you are interested in showing the paths that visitors take through your Web site, you do not need to know the count of each node. Right-click the workspace, and from the pop-up menu select

| Nodes | ▶ | Size | ▶ | None |

All of the nodes are now the same size.

Because the data set uses a sequence variable, the links have direction. Select the following from the pop-up menu to remove the arrows from the links.

| Links | ▶ | Direction | ▶ | None |

The polar tree view should resemble the following display.

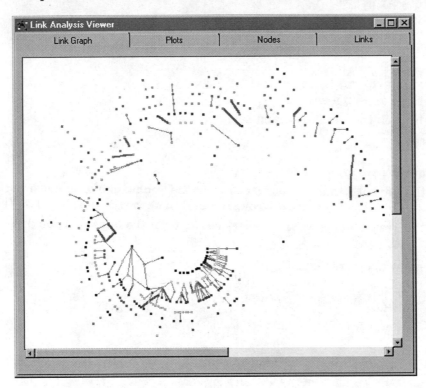

Follow these steps to determine a path between two specific nodes: the traffic between the start-up page (welcome.jsp) and the checkout page (uscheckout.jsp).

1 Right-click the Link Graph workspace and select from the pop-up menu.

| Select | ▶ | Text |

In the Select Text window, select the node **iset1=/apps/pubscat/welcome.jsp**. This is the first instance of the node with welcome.jsp.

2 Right-click the Link Graph workspace and select from the pop-up menu.

| Select | ▶ | Value |

In the Select Value window, select **uscheckout.jsp** and click OK.

3 Right-click the Link Graph workspace and select **Path** from the pop-up menu. The Find Paths window opens.

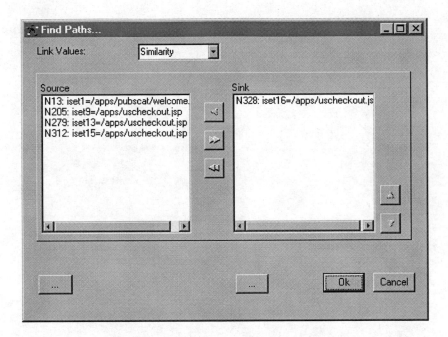

4 In the Source list, select the three nodes that contain welcome.jsp, and move them to the Sink list by clicking the right button (). Click OK.

Examine the contents of the SAS Output window.

```
Path Analysis: Source: N13    Sink: N205

Options: Shortpath Similarity


_from_ _to_        _from_label_                        _to_label_              count


N77   N106  iset4=/apps/pubscat/bookdetails.jsp iset5=/apps/pubscat/bookdetails.jsp   34

N106  N131  iset5=/apps/pubscat/bookdetails.jsp iset6=/apps/pubscat/bookdetails.jsp   31

N131  N162  iset6=/apps/pubscat/bookdetails.jsp iset7=/apps/shopcart.jsp              37

N162  N182  iset7=/apps/shopcart.jsp            iset8=/apps/shopcart.jsp              36

N182  N205  iset8=/apps/shopcart.jsp            iset9=/apps/uscheckout.jsp            37

N13   N26   iset1=/apps/pubscat/welcome.jsp     iset2=/apps/pubscat/bookdetails.jsp   35

N26   N53   iset2=/apps/pubscat/bookdetails.jsp iset3=/apps/pubscat/bookdetails.jsp   21

N53   N77   iset3=/apps/pubscat/bookdetails.jsp iset4=/apps/pubscat/bookdetails.jsp   27
                                                                                    =====
                                                                                      258
```

From this output, you can see that the highest traffic occurs along the following path:

welcome ▶ bookdetails ▶ shopcart ▶ uscheckout.

Some JSPs are reloaded in the path. This path is representative of the overall traffic pattern—it does not indicate that individual visitors traversed the path. In the figure below, you can see that the heaviest traffic occurs in the middle portion of the path, represented by the thick red and blue links. The heaviest traffic indicates that visitors joined and left the path, or that they wandered.

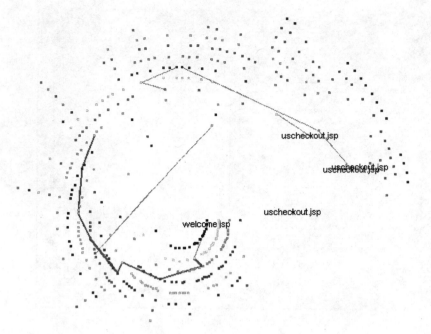

You can also display the overall traffic patterns between each node that contains welcome.jsp and each node that contains uscheckout.jsp. To display the overall traffic pattern,

1 Right-click the Link Graph workspace and select from the pop-up menu.

   | Select | ▶ | Path |

   In the Select Path window, CTRL-click uscheckout.jsp and welcome.jsp.

2 Right-click the Link Graph workspace and select **Path** from the pop-up menu.

3 In the Path window, select the nodes that contain uscheckout.jsp from the Source list, and move them to the Sink list. Click OK.

You can now view the overall traffic patterns between the welcome page and the checkout page.

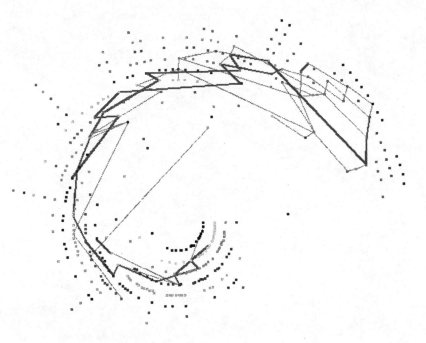

Note again that the thickness and color of the lines indicates nodes that have the heaviest traffic. The information that you obtain from the link graph and from the SAS output enables you to determine where the heaviest traffic exists on your Web site.

APPENDIX

1

Recommended Reading

Recommended Reading

Here is the recommended reading list for this title:

- *Getting Started with SAS Enterprise Miner*
- *SAS/INSIGHT User's Guide*
- *SAS Language Reference: Concepts*

For a complete list of SAS publications, see the current *SAS Publishing Catalog*. To order the most current publications or to receive a free copy of the catalog, contact a SAS representative at

SAS Publishing Sales
SAS Campus Drive
Cary, NC 27513
Telephone: (800) 727-3228*
Fax: (919) 677-8166
E-mail: sasbook@sas.com
Web address: **support.sas.com/pubs**
* For other SAS Institute business, call (919) 677-8000.

Customers outside the United States should contact their local SAS office.

Index

Your Turn

If you have comments or suggestions about *Data Mining Using SAS Enterprise Miner: A Case Study Approach, Second Edition*, please send them to us on a photocopy of this page, or send us electronic mail.

For comments about this book, please return the photocopy to

SAS Publishing
SAS Campus Drive
Cary, NC 27513
email: yourturn@sas.com

For suggestions about the software, please return the photocopy to

SAS Institute Inc.
Technical Support Division
SAS Campus Drive
Cary, NC 27513
email: suggest@sas.com